FOOD

FROM

THE

FIRE

NIKLAS EKSTEDT

FOOD
FROM
THE
FIRE

PHOTOGRAPHY BY
MAX AND LIZ HAARALA HAMILTON

PAVILION

FOR MY SONS, VINSTON AND JOHN, WHO ALWAYS MAKE ME SMILE!

First published in the United Kingdom in 2016 by Pavilion
An imprint of HarperCollinsPublishers
1 London Bridge Street
London SE1 9GF

www.harpercollins.co.uk

HarperCollinsPublishers
Macken House
39/40 Mayor Street Upper
Dublin 1
D01 C9W8
Ireland

ISBN: 978-1-91090-434-3

This book contains FSC™ certified paper and other controlled sources to ensure responsible forest management.
For more information visit: www.harpercollins.co.uk/green

A CIP catalogue record for this book
is available from the British Library.

10

Reproduction by Mission Productions Ltd.
Printed and bound in China by RR Donnelley APS

www.pavilionbooks.com

Publisher's Acknowledgements
Commissioning editor: Emily Preece-Morrison
Photography: Max and Liz Haarala Hamilton
Design direction: Laura Russell
Design: Arielle Gamble
Recipe development and on-location
shoot assistance: Thomas Eidefors
Copy editor: Maggie Ramsay
Indexer: Vanessa Bird

CONTENTS

ON EKSTEDT

I spent the summer of 2011 with my family, in our summer cabin on the island of Ingarö in the Stockholm archipelago. My wife Katarina had just had our first child, our son Vinston, and the idea was that I should have some time away from work. But although I was meant to be a family man on holiday, my head was still in work mode. I had recently signed the contract to open a new restaurant, in Stockholm's exclusive Östermalm district, but I had no idea what to do with it.

I had always thought that I would be settled by the time I had children; that I would mostly oversee the fantastic restaurant empire that I had built up. It hadn't turned out that way. I was 33 years old, and in the eyes of the media and the general public I was 'Food Niklas', a whimsical TV chef without any proper qualifications. It was time to do something big. It was now or never.

I grew up in Järpen, a small village in the province of Jämtland in the north of Sweden. Like most young people, before I could connect with my roots I first needed to turn my back on them. When I trained to become a chef, we were taught to believe that Scandinavia didn't produce good ingredients. I became passionate about Italian olive oil and French braised chicken. When I opened my first restaurant, at the age of 21, I went for super-trendy molecular gastronomy, serving dishes such as 'asparagus clouds'. I could hardly have got any further away from the rustic slow cooking of the Jämtland forests. Now I wanted to reconnect with my roots.

But how should I approach this? New Nordic cuisine already had its poster boys. Magnus Nilsson, who grew up a stone's throw away from me, had set up Fäviken, a top-class restaurant with food inspired by the seasons and ingredients from the forest. René Redzepi, with whom I worked when I was a youngster, has been hugely successful with the same concept at Noma, the Copenhagen restaurant that has been named Best Restaurant in the World several times. I wanted to add my own personal touch to the new Nordic cuisine; copying René or Magnus wouldn't cut it. I wandered around on the island and pondered, like a gloomy character from some black and white Ingmar Bergman film. I stood for ages, just staring at the trees.

Later, I realized I hadn't seen the wood for the trees. Literally.

I thought about building a barbecue, but never got round to it. Instead I chopped down some of the birches I had stared at, so that I had some wood. Then I made a fire pit, like the ones I had made with my parents when I was young and we went to the mountains. That fire pit became our family kitchen that summer – it never went out. Most of the time we grilled in the usual way, on a grill grate, but one day I didn't have enough patience to wait for the fire to burn down to embers, so I whacked a cast-iron pan into the flames. The fire sizzled and sparked around the pan; the force of the heat knocked me back; and the flavours of the food … what depth! Finally I felt like I was on to something.

I started thinking about *asado*, the barbecuing technique from South America. Grilling over open fires was the core of the concept, just as wood-fired ovens were once the core of Swedish cooking. The first penny dropped. Before the arrival of the electric cooker, fire, wood and iron were the holy trinity of the Swedish kitchen. Aha! What if you could combine typical Nordic ingredients with the typical Nordic way of cooking? It would be the perfect way to complete the new Nordic cuisine concept.

Chance helped me along further. We were building a driveway outside our house, so I cut down a juniper bush that was in the way. When I threw the juniper branches onto the fire, the food developed another dimension. The discoveries succeeded each other and I, by this time properly excited, made excuses to go food shopping every day. 'Darling, I forgot to buy marmalade yesterday so I'm just going down to the shops.' Then I would drive the four kilometres, stopping to phone authorities, chefs, suppliers, floor staff and oven builders.

The image of an analogue fine-dining restaurant developed, a place where everything was cooked over fire, like in the old days. My biggest headache was whether it was actually possible. Thor Heyerdahl must have felt the same worry ahead of the Kon-Tiki expedition. How on earth is this raft supposed to float? Who should I take on board with me? I needed established chefs who dared risk their reputation in a stone-age kitchen. My first recruit was Gustav Otterberg, a promising young chef who shared my love for fire. We met at a party and were soon jotting down wood oven sketches on the back of cocktail napkins. Together we went to the Royal Library in Stockholm and devoured cookbooks from the 18th century. To our excitement, we found some fantastic instructional books on how Swedish food was prepared before the advent of electricity.

The idea was, then, to give these ancient techniques a renaissance in my restaurant. Logistically it was pure idiocy – I realized that pretty much straight away. The premises at Humlegårdsgatan had once housed a pizzeria, so pipes for a wood-fired oven were in place, but that was the only thing in my favour. Ventilation was the biggest problem – there was no natural draft, no extraction, there was smoke everywhere! The dry cleaners next door to the restaurant complained that their newly cleaned clothes smelled like a scout camp. Fan motors blew up almost every day. The chefs were pulling their hair out. The heat was far higher than in a modern restaurant kitchen with induction hobs and small copper pans. The ingredients burned up in the pans. What should a wood oven for the modern kitchen look like? We built a stone-age microwave oven: a cast-iron box with glowing embers at the bottom. By placing damp juniper branches on top, we managed to control the heat. Step by step we were getting there.

Had I made it too complicated for myself? Once the guests had been served their food, surely they wouldn't give a damn if it was cooked over an open fire or not. One day a food writer from *Dagens Nyheter* called me up for an interview. The next day I read the headline in the paper: 'Food Niklas opens new grill'. Shit, I thought. If a journalist from the biggest newspaper in the country doesn't understand what I'm trying to do, how will the guests get it?

The first week, the guests all focused on the smoke. 'How smoky does it actually get?' a lady asked. 'I need to know whether to leave my fur coat at home tonight.' Shortly afterwards, a food blogger compared Ekstedt to Aifur, the Viking-themed restaurant owned by the Euro-techno artist E-type. I felt desperate. For the first time in my career I had created something that was one hundred per cent mine. And no one understood.

Luckily, it all turned around. The Swedish food writer Jonas Cramby was probably the first one to get it. In a review in the newspaper *Metro*, he described the experience as a 'food orgasm without electricity'. That review was followed by other accolades. The restaurant guide Zagat named us one of the world's ten most interesting restaurants, and in March 2013 a lifelong dream came true. We received a star in the Michelin Guide. I had succeeded.

At the same time, I felt I had failed. By opening Ekstedt, I'd contributed to the image of the new Nordic cuisine as unachievable snobbery. Home cooks who have seen me pose with a flambadou, a cone-shaped tool that we use at Ekstedt to drip burning fat over rotating chunks of meat, can't imagine doing this at home. But in reality, Nordic cuisine can be summarized by a few techniques and tricks that are easy to get the hang of. Anyone can make their own pickles, anyone can handle a cast-iron pan. With this book, I want to show how Nordic cuisine works in everyday life – in both the home kitchen and outdoors – because that is where it belongs.

Smokily warm greetings, *Niklas Ekstedt*

How to build an open fire pit

HOW TO BUILD
AN OPEN FIRE PIT

1 WHERE TO BUILD THE FIRE PIT

Build your fire in a place where it is open and there is no risk of grass, shrubs or drooping branches catching fire. The fireplace should be about 50–70cm/1½–3ft in diameter.

2 PREPARE THE GROUND

Sweep an area clear of dry grass and twigs. Build the fireplace with stones that can be packed close together, so that they cover the ground completely.

Many fireplaces are built by putting stones in a ring, or sometimes around a pit dug in the ground. This destroys the ground and there is also a risk of fire taking and spreading in the ground itself, especially on forest floors or peat soils. A raised ring of stones around the fire is good to have as a wind break, and as a support for the grill grate (more on that below [3]). Building a fireplace is rather like a jigsaw puzzle, using abandoned pieces of stone. Look for stones around 10–15cm/4–6in tall. How wide your fireplace should be depends on the size of your grill grate. Start by adding the largest stones close together. Twist and turn in order to find the most stable and most dense solution. Fill the gaps with smaller pieces of stone. Try to build the fireplace base so it slopes slightly toward the middle, so that there is less risk of embers falling out and onto the ground, when lit.

3 PLACE STONES TO SUPPORT THE GRILL GRATE

Depending on the size of the grill grate, place two large stones, or several smaller ones, on one side of the fire pit. In this way, you can keep a fire going on the other side, and feed burning firewood under the grill grate when needed. The grill grate should be placed about 25cm/10in higher than the base of the fire.

4 CHOOSING WOOD FOR FUEL

At the restaurant, we use Swedish birch wood that has been allowed to dry slowly in the sun during the summer. Birch quickly dissipates heat, which makes it easy to control the temperature. Spruce and pine are more difficult to light and contain resin which crackles and emits sparks. More solid woods such as ash, rowan and oak are slightly harder to ignite, but burn at a good, high temperature. However, they are more expensive and there is limited supply.

A practical size for firewood logs is 40cm/16in long, and about 7cm/3in in diameter. As a guide, to cook a meal for four people, you will need about 12–15 logs.

WARNING – No! No! And no again!

Never use painted, glued or stained wood to fuel your fire. It will give off dangerous fumes. Also, avoid using lighter fluid to light your fire as that will give your food a bad taste.

5 HOW TO LIGHT THE FIRE (AND WHAT TO USE)

To light the fire, you need some strips of birch bark, about 10 x 10cm/ 4 x 4in, and two sizes of sticks for kindling. Birch bark is easiest to pull by hand from the logs (alternatively, use newspaper). The smallest size of stick, about 0.5–1cm/¼–½in in diameter, is most easily made by placing a log vertically on a stable surface. By eye, measure out the stick at a corner of the log, apply a sharp knife edge against the top of the log, going with the grain, and, using another log, bang firmly on the knife. You can usually get halfway through the log before it breaks in the middle – it doesn't matter. Get together three handfuls of this smallest stick size. For the next size of stick, chop a couple of logs into 6–8 pieces, about 2.5cm/1in in diameter.

Set two pieces of firewood parallel to each other, about 20cm/8in apart. Place two pieces of birch bark between the logs, then place a handful of the smallest stick size on top.

Now place 3–4 of the larger sticks, diagonally, so that they rest against the logs.

Light the birch bark with a match. If the larger sticks do not catch fire, feed with more birch bark and the smallest kindling sticks. When the larger sticks are burning, you can start to place more logs. You have your cooking fire.

ELEMENTS OF THE ANALOGUE KITCHEN

ON WOOD

The sound I remember most clearly from my childhood is the sound of my dad's axe hitting a piece of wood on the chopping block. That hollow sound echoing through the woods. For my dad, chopping and stacking wood was a point of honour. For other Swedish dads, it was even more than that. My friend's father bought cars that he did up and sold on. When he was inspecting a car he always took a good look at the seller's wood pile. If it was neatly stacked he assumed that the car was in good condition. If the pieces of wood were all spread out in the melting snow under some mouldy tarpaulin ... no deal!

We Scandinavians are tree huggers. Or, more accurately, we are obsessed with trees and wood. According to Norse mythology, the first people in the world came from the tree Yggdrasil, and trees were for a millennia a prerequisite for life in our part of the world. If we ran out of wood, we ran out of life. There are other countries that have a wood-fired food culture, but we used the wood for both heating our houses and for cooking. First, we made a fire in the wood-fired stove in order not to die from the cold, and then we slow-cooked our food using the residual heat, in order not to die from hunger. By the way, the answer is no, I'm not the one who chops all the wood at Ekstedt. Unfortunately. At the restaurant we use a cubic metre of wood a day, so our only option is to buy ready-chopped wood from Norrland (the northern half of Sweden). Birch wood from the north burns reliably, giving off a high, even heat. Fir and pine, on the other hand, don't burn well: they crackle and give off sparks.

But wood isn't just for making a fire, it is also great for adding flavour. The classic Swedish woods – pine, fir and birch – don't work well for smoking; for this purpose we use juniper. At Ekstedt we use whole branches that have been dampened before they go onto the embers. You can do this at home too. Place some wet juniper stems onto the embers in your barbecue, kettle grill or smoker, and the fish or meat will taste as if they've come from a top restaurant. You can also save and dry twigs from fruit trees such as apple, pear, plum and cherry, to add a fantastic flavour to the smoked ingredient. The food industry has woken up to the trend and you can now even buy smoke flavouring in

bottled liquid form. But remember – just because you don't like the flavour of cheap hickory imitations, that doesn't mean that you don't like smoked food. Try the real deal some day.

Of course, you don't have to chop your own wood – like I said, I don't – but I recommend having a go if you get the opportunity. If only to take part in what still is the sport of sports among Swedish men. Even though wood isn't a prerequisite for survival any more, the art of chopping wood seems to be something that a lot of people dream of mastering. Just look at fashion trends: people who want to look cool dress like lumberjacks, even if they live in the city. In Sweden, chopping wood has become a hobby, a way to compensate for sitting at your desk all day, with palms that carry no trace of calluses. Every bank executive in this country drives out to their cabin and chops wood in the holidays. And I hope that they cook food over the fire afterwards.

ON FIRE

Let's start by setting an old misconception alight. Cooking food with fire is not the same as cooking food over the fire. At Ekstedt we have several fire sources: an open fire, a wood-fired stove, a smoker, a fire pit and a 'stone-age microwave oven', which is an ember-filled box warmed with smoke funnelled from the main fire pit. We dip into fire, we grill over embers, we chimney smoke, we drip burning fat over whole cuts of meat using a flambadou … The fire touches every dish. Every evening someone comments on the smoke smell that permeates the dining room. Everyone says the same thing: 'Ah, it smells like my childhood!'

During my own childhood, all activities finished with a fire. Mountain walks, canoeing trips and journeys on the snowmobile … Whatever we did always ended up with us making a fire. But as a young chef, when I tried to analyse what I stood for in terms of cooking, I was certainly not looking back towards the fires of my childhood. A sophisticated Swede has always been an outward-looking Swede. But I'm glad that I started to look inwards again. When we opened Ekstedt I got, for the first time, an understanding of the foundations of Swedish gastronomy. Some things had to be slow-cooked out of necessity, using the residual heat of the wood-fired oven. And it's not delicate, like Asian cooking. There it's all about finely shredded vegetables sizzling away in the pan and ready in one minute. The shredded veg would just burst into flames if we did that. We shove whole salsify into the flames instead. That's more how we roll.

In a way the whole Ekstedt concept – analogue cooking – is playing with fire. We're swaggering around in welding aprons, lugging piles of wood through the dining room. It's an enormously long way down should we fall. My greatest fear is to be reduced to a gimmick. If it says 'ember-grilled' on the menu, it should bloody well taste ember-grilled. Otherwise, it all just turns into the story of the emperor's new clothes. Luckily, fire adds to the food. I promise. The fire adds flavour, character and attitude. Cooking with fire means that you become more aware as a cook. You have to master two living things: the fire and the ingredient. For me, cooking is like music, it's completely different when you do it unplugged.

ON SMOKE

In the Nordic countries there is no standard smoke flavour, instead every family has their own 'signature smoke', and most people encounter smoked foods very early in life. When I serve smoked fish at the restaurant, guests always mention their early childhood memories; harkening back to times spent on the archipelago or to fires by the lakes in the north.

It's important to make use of freshly caught fish as quickly as possible, and smoking it in a homemade smoke box is common here. Different techniques are used and discussed frequently; could it be Grandad's or Dad's method that is the absolute best? Everyone has their own personal preference for how the finished result should taste. Usually an ingredient will be cured for a day or two before the actual smoking process begins. Salting the meat or fish slightly before smoking means it also keeps fresh for a considerably longer amount of time. Apart from using smoke to keep food fresh for longer, I also use it for flavouring.

When cooking, I mostly use birch wood to get the best embers, the absolutely hottest fire or the perfect temperature in the wood-fired oven. But when I smoke food, it's a bit different. Birch is not the ultimate wood for smoking; instead I would recommend wood from fruit trees or juniper bushes.

Choose from a range of different woods depending on what you are cooking. Alder has a very mild smoke flavour that goes well with salmon or herring and is fantastic for smoking pork. Both pear and apple are fantastic to use for all types of smoking. A tip is to save branches and twigs when you prune fruit trees in spring, and leave them to dry slightly. Some people remove the bark from the wood, but I haven't noticed any difference to the end result, so as far as I'm concerned, anything goes. Another tip is to use chips from oak mixed together with some juniper berries, which will add extra flavour. There is a plethora of different woods and wood chips to choose from, and of course you'll just have to try them and see what works for you. In this book, I mostly use wood from fruit trees as I've got them growing in my own back garden.

ON CAST IRON

In Sweden, when someone moves away from home, it's a tradition to give them a cast-iron pot. That really says something, in my opinion. When we are expected to stand on our own two feet, we're given a kitchen utensil made from cast iron. Many of us associate the smell of fire and cast iron with childhood. When I was little, the cast-iron pot came out to cook elk stew or sautéed reindeer. We had a wood-fired stove made of cast iron in my childhood home in Järpen, but it was only used for heating. We cooked food on the electric cooker, just like everyone else. The wood-fired stove stood there like a monument to a gastronomy long gone.

Swedes are early adopters, which in most cases is a positive thing. When electricity had its big breakthrough the change happened with record speed. Yay, all of a sudden we no longer had to lug wood around in the biting wind. Our gastronomy that had developed in harmony with cast iron was thrown out. It happened quickly, too quickly. We forgot our roots.

When I went to cookery school in Åre, cast iron was hopelessly out of fashion. We used stainless steel, sous vide… anything except cast iron. Cast iron was for farmers, a museum artefact that was said to ruin the food. If you cooked anything acidic in the pans, you released so much iron that the food tasted of nosebleed. We completely denied our cultural heritage.

Luckily, I would come to rediscover cast iron. In 2011, I heard that Simon Blomgren, a highly respected businessman, had bought Skeppshult, a classic old company that makes cast-iron kitchen utensils. At that time I sensed that cast iron had a future after all. Shortly afterwards, the idea to open Ekstedt took form, an analogue restaurant where cast iron would play a major role.

When using cast iron, you get a heat that is more concentrated. You get a thicker and more even crust, not just a thin crisp coat. But it's more than just a texture changer. A cast-iron pan retains the heat much better too. If you are cooking a piece of fish, for example, you can remove the pan from the heat and leave the fish to finish cooking in the pan. A standard pan will lose its heat quickly; you would have to put it in the the oven to finish cooking the fish. But the best thing about cast iron is that it fundamentally changes the ingredients. An onion finds its soulmate in cast iron. You can only really caramelize an onion in a cast-iron pan. When humble vegetables such as onion and tomato meet cast iron, they get added oomph, an umami-like flavour boost.

I remember one evening, a few days before we opened the restaurant, Gustav Otterberg, one of our chefs, called me and sounded excited: 'You have to come over and try this lobster that I've cooked. Now.' The combination of smoke, fat and acidity made everything spin. In all seriousness, I felt dizzy. At Ekstedt, all the dishes have touched cast iron, either during the *mise en place* or during service. Without cast iron, our restaurant couldn't exist. The cast-iron ovens and pans are our regulators. Without them, we would have only two options: raw or burnt to smithereens.

When you start cooking in a cast-iron pan or pot, just watch out that you don't go over the top with enthusiasm, as I did. When I rediscovered cast iron, I went completely bananas. I made Indian curries, Mexican stews, Bolognese sauce ... something was always simmering away in the cast-iron pot. When we went to see the midwife, my wife Katarina was complimented on her exemplary iron levels. That was nice, of course, but everything has its limits. When she went to the maternity unit to give birth to John, I brought some Indian curry that I had made in my beloved pot. Katarina glared at me and said: 'I'd actually rather eat the hospital food.'

ON FAT

When I took part in a food event in Copenhagen a few years ago, I was told that it was the Vikings who invented butter. They brought butter with them when they travelled to faraway countries and, one day, landing in Normandy in France, they taught the French the art of culturing and churning the perfect butter. Perhaps this is a myth or a patriotic Nordic view of the small, fat, golden yellow lump that we love so much, but butter is an important part of our food culture.

Butter can easily burn at high temperatures, so it is complicated to use it for cooking in the way that I do, directly over fire. However, I often use it for flavouring. The butter recipe I give on page 56 is a lot easier to make at home than you might think. If you're lucky enough to be able to source an exceptionally good-quality cream or unpasteurised milk directly from a farmer, this will be a butter that's one of a kind.

Other fats I make use of are tallow and lard. Tallow is fat rendered from beef, and lard is from pork. They are both solid at room temperature and have a very high smoke point, so they're great for frying, but I also like to set the fat alight in a *flambadou* and use it to flash-cook or baste meats.

A *flambadou*, also called a *flamboir à lard*, is a thick iron cone mounted at the end of a long handle. It is traditionally used with rotisserie cooking, where burning lard or tallow, dripped from the cone of the *flambadou*, crisps the skin of the roasting meat. Cooking thinly sliced meat, fish or seafood by this method lightly sears the ingredient and gives a delicious smoky character to the food. They are not widely available, but can be sourced online (see page 237 for some suppliers).

To use, allow the *flambadou* to become red hot in the embers of the fire. Once hot, insert a piece of lard or tallow into the cone. The fat will ignite and you can then drip it over thinly cut meat or fish to flash-cook it, or to give it golden, crispy skin in the case of roasting meat, thereby keeping it succulent and giving it a unique flavour.

Worth keeping in mind is that fats absorbs a lot of smoke flavour – that's why bacon tastes so strong, for example. So try it out yourself and be a bit careful to start off with, and you will soon find the note that is right for you!

BASICS

SALTS, SPICE MIXES AND PICKLES

HAY SALT

Burned hay combined with salt adds a delicate smoky flavour to fish, meat and vegetables. I buy organic hay from a local pet store for this purpose.

Makes approx. 55g/2oz

1 bunch of fresh, clean, dry hay
   (approx. 4 big handfuls)
55g/2oz/3 tbsp sea salt

Place the hay in a fire-resistant tray or a cast-iron pan and set the hay on fire. Make sure all the hay is burned to ash.

Tip the hay ash into a mortar, add the salt and grind together.

Sift through a fine sieve and store in an airtight container.

ROSÉ PEPPER SALT

Great to serve on the side to complement grilled beef or lamb.

Makes approx. 60g/2oz

1 tsp pink peppercorns
55g/2oz/3 tbsp sea salt

Roast the peppercorns in a dry pan over medium heat for about 5 minutes, stirring constantly. Set aside and leave to cool.

Combine the salt and peppercorns in a mortar and grind together. Store in an airtight container.

CITRUS SALT

This is great with grilled fish.

Makes approx. 85g/3oz

85g/3oz/4½ tbsp sea salt
1 tsp finely chopped dried citrus peel (see page 54)

Combine the salt and citrus peel in a mortar and grind together. Store in an airtight container.

CURING SALT AND SUGAR MIX

Marinated salmon or *gravad* ('buried') salmon is a typical dish on the Swedish *smörgåsbord* at celebrations for Christmas, Easter and midsummer. The term *gravad* derives from medieval times, when fish such as cod, salmon and trout were rubbed with salt and buried in the ground, resulting in a kind of fermentation that preserved the fish. Today we marinate fish in this curing mixture and store it in the refrigerator for 3–5 days.

You can make this in advance, omitting the dill, and it will keep for 6 months in an airtight container. Add the fresh dill just before using. This quantity will be enough to cure 3–4 fillets of fish, about 1.8kg/4lb.

Makes approx. 75g/2¾oz

45g/1½oz/2½ tbsp sea salt
½ tsp black peppercorns
30g/1oz/2 tbsp caster (superfine) sugar
2 tsp finely chopped fresh dill

Combine the salt and peppercorns and sugar in a mortar and grind together. Store in an airtight container. Stir in the dill just before using.

PICKLING LIQUID 1-2-3

A Swedish feast cannot be without pickles. Pickling was historically an important way to preserve the harvest before the winter in Sweden. Ättika is a strong Swedish white (clear) vinegar that is traditionally used for preserving. 1-2-3 refers to the proportions of vinegar, sugar and water, and this recipe is the basis for many pickled vegetables and fish. A Swedish feast cannot be without pickles.

In many countries the white distilled vinegar used for pickling is less concentrated (5–8%); if using this type of vinegar, the proportions of the recipe change to 2-2-2 – in other words, use more vinegar and less water.

Makes approx. 2.5 litres/4½ pints/10 cups

450ml/16fl oz/2 cups 10–12% ättika (Swedish white vinegar)
900g/2lb/5 cups sugar
1.4 litres/2½ pints/6 cups water
1 tsp black peppercorns
3 bay leaves

Combine all the ingredients in a large pan and bring to the boil. Stir until the sugar has dissolved.

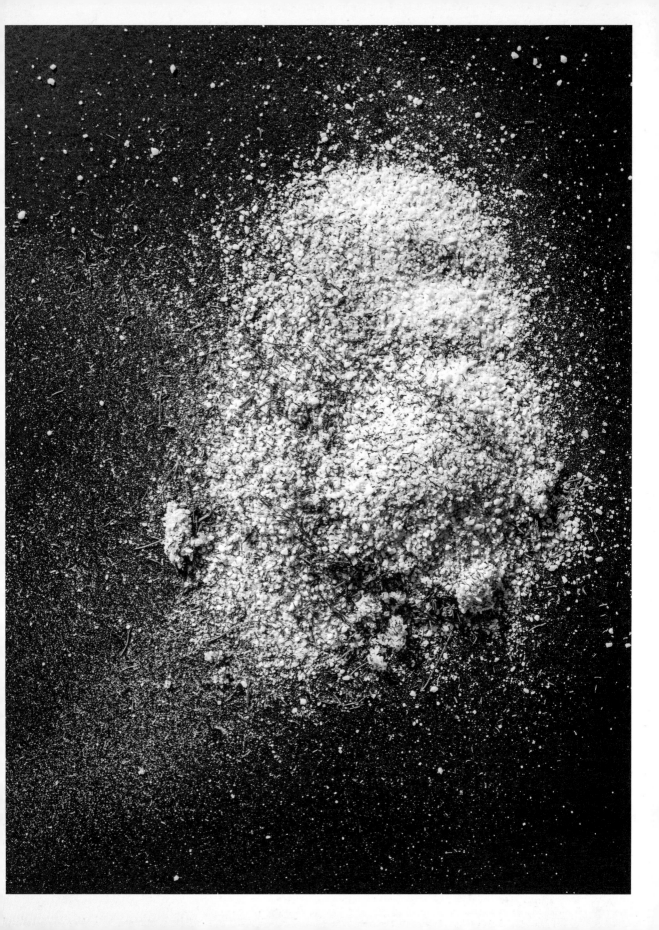

SKÅNSK MUSTARD

The traditional mustard from Skåne, the southernmost county of Sweden. It used to be made in a bowl with a cannonball to grind the seeds, but thankfully works just as well with a stick mixer or food processor.

At the Swedish Christmas dinner table, a baked ham with a mustard crust is a must. And a sweet honey mustard makes a great condiment for grilled sausages, cured hams or smoked fish. Simply combine 2 parts mustard with 1 part honey.

Makes approx. 200ml / 7fl oz / generous ¾ cup

30g / 1oz / 3 tbsp yellow mustard seeds
30g / 1oz / 3 tbsp brown mustard seeds
100ml / 3½fl oz / ½ cup water
2 tsp white wine vinegar
2 tbsp honey
½ tsp salt
1 tbsp vegetable oil
½ tsp dried tarragon
2 tsp cognac

Put the mustard seeds and water in a saucepan and bring to the boil over medium heat. Set aside for 10 minutes.

Put all the ingredients into a food processor and mix to a smooth paste. If needed, you can add a little more water. Pour into sterilized jars, seal, and store in a cool, dark place for up to 6 months.

PRESERVED FRUIT, VEGETABLES AND FLOWERS

Many different methods of preservation are used all over the world to store ingredients so they can be eaten out of season. In Sweden, pickled vegetables, fruit and herring are particularly popular. The following recipes are some of my favourites and preserve ingredients that have very short seasons.

PICKLED RAMSON BUDS

Look for the white flowers of ramsons, also known as wild garlic, in woodlands in the springtime.

Makes about 300g / 10½oz

225g / 8oz freshly picked ramson buds
225ml / 8fl oz / scant 1 cup pickling liquid 1-2-3
  (see page 40), cooled
1 tsp salt

Rinse the buds in cold water and drain on paper towels.

Combine all the ingredients in a sterilized jar and cover the surface with clingfilm to prevent oxidation. Seal tightly and store in a cold place for 3 days before serving. They will keep for up to 6 months.

PICKLED GOOSEBERRIES

Makes about 2kg/4½lb

1.1kg/2½lb/7½ cups gooseberries, topped
   and tailed
120ml/4fl oz/½ cup ättika (Swedish white vinegar)
   or 240ml/8fl oz/1 cup white distilled vinegar
450g/1lb/2¼ cups caster (superfine) sugar
450ml/16fl oz/2 cups water
1 fresh red chilli, deseeded and cut in half
1 tbsp yellow mustard seeds
2 tsp salt

Rinse the gooseberries in cold water.

Put all the other ingredients in a saucepan and
bring to the boil until the sugar has dissolved.

Add the gooseberries and bring back to the boil.
Place in a sterilized jar, cover and leave to cool.

Store in a cold place for 3 days before serving.
They will keep for up to 1 year.

PICKLED RHUBARB

Makes about 1kg/2lb

700g/1½lb rhubarb, peeled and chopped
900ml/32fl oz/3¾ cups pickling liquid 1-2-3
   (see page 40)
1 tbsp fennel seeds
2 tsp salt

Put the rhubarb in a sterilized jar.

Bring the pickling liquid, fennel seeds and salt to
the boil. Pour the warm liquid over the rhubarb.
Cover and leave to cool.

Store in a cold place for 3 days before serving.
It will keep for up to 6 months.

PRESERVED RHUBARB

This is best made with tender young rhubarb. If you are using older rhubarb, cook the pieces in the syrup until soft, about 6–8 minutes.

Makes about 1.2kg / 2½lb

900g / 2lb rhubarb
450ml / 16fl oz / 2 cups water
450g / 1lb / 2¼ cups caster (superfine) sugar
3 tbsp freshly squeezed lemon juice
3 cardamom pods

Peel the rhubarb and keep the skin. Cut lengthways into pieces about 5mm / ¼in wide (the length of the pieces depends on the size of the jar) and place in a sterilized jar.

Put the rhubarb skin in a saucepan with the water, sugar, lemon juice and cardamom and bring to the boil. Stir until the sugar has dissolved.

Strain the liquid over the rhubarb, cover and leave to cool.

Store in a cold place for 3 days before serving. This will keep for up to 6 months.

PRESERVED REDCURRANTS

Redcurrants or blackcurrants work equally well in this recipe. Redcurrants make a great alternative to lingonberries to serve with Swedish meatballs.

Makes about 1.5kg / 3½lb

1.3kg / 3lb / 11 cups redcurrants
1 red chilli, deseeded and finely chopped
120ml / 4fl oz / ½ cup water
50ml / 2fl oz / 3 tbsp ättika (Swedish white vinegar), or 120ml / 4fl oz / ½ cup white distilled vinegar
70g / 2½oz / ⅔ cup caster (superfine) sugar
1 cinnamon stick
6 cloves
1 tbsp finely chopped fresh ginger

Rinse the redcurrants in cold water and remove the stems.

Combine all the ingredients in a wide saucepan over a low heat, bring slowly to the boil and simmer for 10 minutes.

Remove from the heat and leave to cool. Pour into a sterilized jar and store in a cold place for 3 days before serving. This will keep for up to 6 months.

PICKLED ELDERBERRIES

During June in Sweden, we commonly make lemonade with elderflowers, sugar and lemon. When the berries mature in September and October, pickling is a great way of preserving some of that summer freshness to last us through the dark Swedish winter. Use in salads or as an accompaniment to stews or soup.

Makes about 2.5kg / 5½lb

40 bunches of elderberries
2.25 litres / 4 pints / 9½ cups pickling liquid 1-2-3
   (see page 40), cooled

Rinse the elderberries in cold water and drain on paper towels.

Put them in a large sterilized jar, cover with pickling liquid, then cover the surface with clingfilm to prevent oxidation. Seal tightly.

Store in a cold place for 3 days before serving. They will keep for up to 6 months.

CURRY PICKLES

This is great at a barbecue as a spicy condiment for roasted chicken, or grilled turbot with lemons (see page 158).

Makes approx. 1.8kg / 4lb

4 yellow beetroots
55g / 2oz / 3 tbsp salt
1 green courgette (zucchini)
1 white onion, peeled
1 tsp each black and yellow mustard seeds
1 bay leaf
1 tbsp curry powder
1 tsp ground turmeric
1.4 litres / 2½ pints / 6 cups water
700ml / 1¼ pints / 3 cups cider vinegar
225g / 8oz / generous 1 cup caster (superfine) sugar

Clean the beetroots in cold water. Place in a saucepan, cover with water and add 2 tablespoons of salt. Bring to the boil over medium heat and cook until just tender. Turn off the heat and leave to cool in the water. Peel the beetroots and cut into 2cm / ¾in wedges; set aside.

Cut the courgette and onion into fine slices. Combine with 1 tablespoon of salt in a bowl and leave for 30 minutes. Rinse the courgette and onion in cold water and drain.

Put the spices, water, vinegar and sugar in a pan and bring to the boil, stirring until the sugar has dissolved. Pack the beetroots, courgette and onion tightly in a sterilized container. Pour over the hot pickling liquid, cover with a lid and leave to cool.

Store in the refrigerator for 2 days before serving. They will keep for up to 3 weeks.

PICKLED VEGETABLES

When home-grown and local vegetables are ripe and at their best, you sometimes have more than you know what to do with. That's when you pickle! This way, you can enjoy good vegetables for the rest of the year.

Makes approx. 1.3kg / 3lb

½ pointed cabbage
½ cauliflower
2 carrots, peeled
1 litre / 1¾ pints / 1 quart water
55g / 2oz / 3 tbsp salt
1.4 litres / 2½ pints / 6 cups pickling liquid 1-2-3
  (see page 40)
1 tbsp caraway seeds

Cut out the central cores of the cabbage and cauliflower. Cut the cabbage leaves and cauliflower florets into roughly 2cm / ¾in pieces. Slice the carrots into 3mm / ⅛in slices.

Bring the water and salt to the boil in a pan. Add the vegetables and simmer for 3 minutes. Drain and rinse in cold running water; drain in a colander.

Bring the pickling liquid and caraway seeds to the boil. Set aside and keep warm. Pack the vegetables tightly in a sterilized container. Pour over the hot pickling liquid, cover with a lid, and leave to cool.

Store in the refrigerator for 2 days before serving. They will keep for up to 3 weeks.

DRIED CITRUS PEEL

Dried Seville orange is a typical spice used in *glögg* at Christmas time (see page 228). Alternatively you can use it to make citrus salt (see page 36), or grind the peel and sprinkle over fish, meat or game casseroles. It also makes a nice garnish for desserts or hot chocolate (see page 220).

Makes approx. 55g / 2oz

2 oranges
2 lemons
2 Seville oranges

Preheat the oven to 80°C / 175°F (the lowest possible setting).

Clean the fruits in cold water and dry on paper towels. Using a vegetable peeler, peel the skin in large pieces and trim off the white pith.

Spread the citrus peel on a baking sheet and dry in the oven for about 2 hours.

Store in an airtight container at room temperature.

DAIRY

HOMEMADE BUTTER

It's really easy to make your own butter.
Save the whey (buttermilk) for baking bread
or making your own sour cream cheese
(see page 61).

Makes approx. 200g/7oz

900ml/32fl oz/3¾ cups double (heavy) cream
90ml/3fl oz/6 tbsp sour cream
1 tsp sea salt

Combine the cream and sour cream in a bowl
and mix gently until smooth. Cover and leave at
room temperature for about 24 hours. It will taste
slightly sour.

Chill the liquid to about 10°C/50°F. Using an
electric whisk on medium speed, beat the liquid
until it separates and you see pale yellow lumps in
the buttermilk.

With very clean hands, squeeze the yellow lumps
together, squeezing out the buttermilk. Work the
butter as long as you want: the more buttermilk
is squeezed out, the fatter and more durable the
butter will be. But at the same time, you will
lose some acidity and pleasant aromas. I generally
prefer a shorter processing time, but if I want a
butter that will keep for up to 30 days, I squeeze
out as much as possible of the buttermilk, then add
some cold water and process the butter again until
all water has been squeezed. Season with salt to
taste. Cover and store in the refrigerator.

JUNIPER BUTTER

Serve with venison, beef or pork, or
with vegetables such as cabbage or globe
artichokes (see page 88).

Makes approx. 85g/3oz

85g/3oz salted butter
2 juniper berries, crushed

Melt the butter in a saucepan over medium
heat. Add the crushed juniper and increase the
heat. When the butter begins to simmer, start
whisking constantly. This will prevent particles
settling on the bottom and getting burned. Keep
stirring until the butter is light brown. Remove
the pan from the heat before the butter burns.
Pour the butter into a bowl.

Use fresh, or cover and store in the refrigerator
for up to 1 month.

BROWN BUTTER

This butter has a unique nutty flavour.
Season with salt and vinegar and you have
a delicious sauce, or use it in an emulsion such
as brown butter mayonnaise (see page 115).

Makes approx. 85g / 3oz

85g / 3oz / 6 tbsp salted butter

Melt the butter in a saucepan over medium heat.

Increase the heat until the butter begins to simmer,
then start whisking constantly. This will prevent
particles settling on the bottom and getting
burned. Keep stirring until the butter is light
brown. Remove the pan from the heat before the
butter burns. Pour the butter into a bowl.

Use fresh, or cover and store in the refrigerator for
up to 1 month.

SMOKED BUTTER

Serve this as a sauce with grilled fish or meat,
or use to flavour mashed potato.

Makes approx. 85g / 3oz

115g / 4oz smoking chips or a stem of juniper
85g / 3oz / 6 tbsp butter or brown butter (see recipe
    opposite), at room temperature

Light up a smoker with your choice of smoking
chips or a stem of juniper.

Put the butter in a heat-resistant jug or pan and
place in the smoker for about 20 minutes. Do not
let the temperature go above 100°C / 210°F.

Use fresh, or leave to cool and store, covered, in
the refrigerator for up to 1 month.

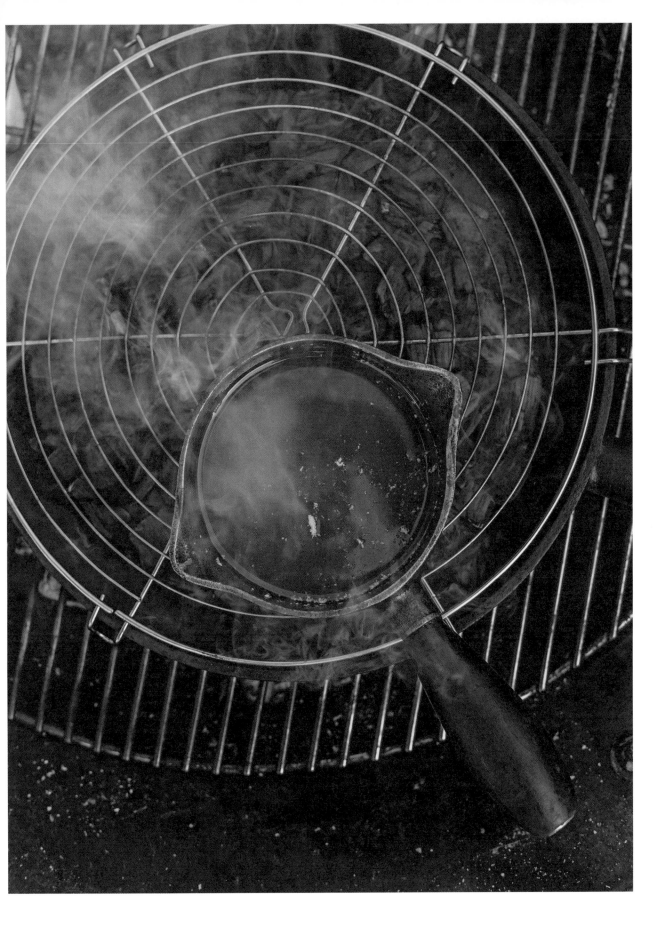

FRESH CHEESE

If you have extra milk and don't want it to spoil and go to waste, make fresh cheese!

Makes approx. 400g / 14oz

450ml / 16fl oz / 2 cups whole milk
225ml / 8fl oz / scant 1 cup double (heavy) cream
3 rhubarb stalks, cut in half lengthways
½ tsp salt

Bring the milk and cream to the boil in a saucepan. Remove from the heat and add the rhubarb and salt. Cover the surface with clingfilm and leave for 15 minutes.

Put the pan back over low heat and bring to the boil, stirring constantly. Repeat twice. Leave to cool.

Lift out the rhubarb. Strain through cheesecloth over a large bowl to collect the whey, and leave to drain for 2 hours at room temperature.

Store the cheese in its cheesecloth, covered in whey, in the refrigerator.

FRESH SOUR CREAM CHEESE

Makes approx. 450g / 1lb

650ml / 23fl oz / 2¾ cups whole milk
350ml / 12fl oz / 1½ cups sour cream
1 tsp salt

Bring the milk to the boil in a saucepan. Reduce the heat, add the sour cream and salt, and simmer very gently, stirring constantly, until it separates into curds and whey. Leave to cool.

Strain through cheesecloth over a large bowl to collect the whey, and leave to drain for 2 hours at room temperature.

Store the cheese in its cheesecloth, covered in whey, in the refrigerator.

SPICY FRESH CHEESE

Makes approx. 450g / 1lb

1 tsp caraway seeds
1 tsp fennel seeds
½ tsp paprika
½ tsp dried dill
450g / 1lb / 2 cups fresh sour cream cheese
   (see page 61)

Grind all the spices together in a mortar. Mix with the cheese and season with salt to taste.

Store in the refrigerator.

POTKÄS
POTTED CHEESE

A traditional Scandinavian way of preserving leftover cheese to avoid waste. Serve with crispbread (page 68) or rye bread (page 67).

Makes approx. 450g / 1lb

1 tsp caraway seeds
1 tsp coriander seeds
280g / 10oz hard cheese, such as Cheddar,
   coarsely grated
85g / 3oz / 6 tbsp butter, at room temperature
4 tbsp Madeira wine
½ tsp salt

Roast the caraway and coriander seeds in a dry pan over medium–high heat, then grind them coarsely in a mortar.

Combine the spices with the cheese, butter and Madeira, and mix well with a large spoon. Season with salt to taste. If you like, you could add more spices. Cover and store in the refrigerator for 24 hours before serving.

BREAD

SOURDOUGH BREAD

In the restaurant, we have had the same sourdough starter since 2011. Look after your starter and it will live for a lifetime. You will need to begin preparing the starter 5 days before baking the bread. In this recipe I have added fresh yeast to improve the fermentation.

Makes 2 large loaves

10g/½oz/½ cake fresh yeast
600ml/20fl oz/2½ cups water, at room temperature
900g/2lb/7¼ cups flour, preferably untreated
   organic or stoneground flour
400g/14oz sourdough starter (see below for method)
5 tsp salt

Sourdough starter
400ml/14fl oz/1⅔ cups water, at 36°C/97°F
315g/11oz/2½ cups flour, preferably untreated
   organic or stoneground flour
1 tbsp honey

First make the sourdough starter:

Day 1: Combine 200ml/7fl oz water, 150g/5oz flour and the honey, and whisk to a smooth paste. Cover with a tight lid or clingfilm and store at room temperature for 2 days.

Day 3: Add 100ml/3½fl oz water and 85g/3oz flour to the mixture and mix in well. Cover again and store at room temperature for 24 hours.

Day 4: Add 100ml/3½fl oz water and 85g/3oz flour to the mixture and mix in well. Cover again and store at room temperature for 24 hours.

To make the bread:

Dissolve the yeast in the water. Add half the flour and knead the dough for about 10 minutes.

Add 400g/14oz of the sourdough starter, salt and the remaining flour and knead the dough for 20 minutes.

Put the dough in a large bowl, cover with a cloth and leave to rise for 2 hours.

Pour the dough onto a floured work surface, cut in half and gently shape it into 2 loaves. Avoid overworking the dough; handle it with care to retain as much air as possible. Lightly flour the dough, cover with a cloth and leave to rise for 1½ hours.

Preheat the oven to 250°C/480°F/gas 10.

Turn out the dough onto a baking sheet and place in the oven. Pour 250ml/9fl oz/1 cup of water into a roasting pan in the bottom of the oven (this will make a nice crackly crust).

Turn the oven down to 200°C/400°F/gas 6 and bake for 45–50 minutes, until it sounds hollow when the base is tapped. Leave to cool on a wire rack.

RYE BREAD

The bread typically used for Danish *smørrebrød*, or open sandwiches.

Pictured here with *Potkäs* (see page 62).

Makes 2 loaves

55g/2oz/4 tbsp butter, melted,
   plus 3 tbsp to brush the loaf tins
240g/8½oz/2 cups bread flour
175g/6oz/1½ cups wholewheat (graham) flour
175g/6oz/1¾ cups sifted rye flour
150g/5½oz/1 cup mixed seeds (linseeds,
   crushed rye, sunflower seeds, wheat bran)
4 tsp bicarbonate of soda (baking soda)
1 tsp salt
55g/2oz/3 tbsp dark corn syrup, or golden syrup
450ml/16fl oz/2 cups buttermilk
450ml/16fl oz/2 cups sour cream

Preheat the oven to 180°C/350°F/gas 4. Brush two large loaf tins (with a capacity of about 1.5–2 litres/2½–3½ pints/1½–2 quarts) with melted butter.

Mix the flours, seeds, bicarbonate of soda and salt in a large bowl. Add the melted butter, syrup, buttermilk and sour cream, and mix to a smooth paste. Pour into the loaf tins and bake for 1 hour and 20 minutes until it sounds hollow when the bottom of the loaf is tapped.

Remove from the oven and leave in the tins for 7 minutes. Turn out the bread onto a wire rack, cover with a cloth and leave to cool.

KNÄCKEBRÖD
RYE CRISPBREAD

The most traditional Swedish bread, this is always included in the *smörgåsbord* at Christmas and midsummer celebrations. They were traditionally made with a hole in the centre so that they could be hung over the oven to keep dry. It's up to you whether you want to make the hole or not. It is perfect for sharing, spread simply with butter or cheese.

In the restaurant, we bake bread in a clay oven with an open fire. You can recreate this at home by using a baking stone in a regular oven. The baking stone maintains a high, even temperature. You can either bake directly on the stone or use parchment paper. Preheat the stone for about 45 minutes. When using a baking stone, the cooking time will be halved.

Makes 20 crispbreads

450ml/16fl oz/2 cups milk
40g/1½oz/2 cakes fresh yeast
300g/10½oz/3 cups fine rye flour
55g/2oz/½ cup coarse rye flour
2 tsp salt
370g/13oz/3 cups plain (all-purpose) flour
225g/8oz/2¼ cups coarse rye flour for rolling out
vegetable oil, for brushing the baking sheet

Heat the milk to 37°C/100°F. In a large bowl, mix the milk and yeast, whisking to dissolve the yeast. Mix in the rye flours, salt and finally the wheat flour. Work into a dough until it is not sticking to the bowl. If necessary, add some more coarse rye flour.

Put the dough on a floured work surface, roll into a log and divide into 20 equal pieces. Shape each piece into a bun, cover with a cloth, and leave for 20 minutes.

Preheat the oven to 250°C/480°F/gas 10.

Sprinkle some coarse rye flour on the work surface and roll out each bun, first with a smooth rolling pin and then with a knobbed rolling pin; turn the dough occasionally and roll it out to about 20cm/8in in diameter. The thinner you roll it, the crispier the bread. If you don't have a knobbed rolling pin, you can make a pattern of indentations on the surface of the dough with a fork.

Brush a large baking sheet lightly with oil and carefully add some of the dough circles. You will have to cook them in batches.

Bake for about 5 minutes until lightly browned. Leave to cool on a wire rack.

TUNNBRÖD
FLATBREAD

Back in the days when we relied on watermills to grind grains into flour, the mills depended on the flow of water, which was usually high in spring and autumn; it was useful to make crisp bread that would last for months. Crisp bread is still a major part of a Swede's bread basket: we each eat about 4kg/9lb of this type of bread a year.

Makes 25 flatbreads

450ml/16fl oz/2 cups water
20g/¾oz/1 cake fresh yeast
40g/1½oz/3 tbsp butter
3 tbsp golden syrup or corn syrup
315g/11oz/3 cups fine rye flour
1 tsp salt
400g/14oz/3¼ cups plain (all-purpose) flour, plus extra for dusting
½ tsp ammonium carbonate (baker's ammonium)

Heat the water to 37°C/100°F. In a large bowl, mix the water and yeast, whisking to dissolve the yeast. Add the remaining ingredients and work into a dough until it is not sticking to the bowl. If necessary, add some more wheat flour. Cover with a cloth and leave for 20 minutes.

Preheat the oven to 250°C/480°F/gas 10.

Put the dough on a floured work surface, roll into a log and divide into 25 pieces. Sprinkle some more flour on the work surface and roll each piece into a bun, first with a smooth rolling pin and then with a knobbed rolling pin; turn the dough occasionally and roll it out to about 20cm/8in square. The thinner you roll it, the crispier the bread.

Brush a large baking sheet lightly with oil and carefully add some of the dough squares. You will have to cook them in batches.

Bake for about 3–4 minutes. Leave to cool on a wire rack.

SMALL DISHES

SOURDOUGH TOAST WITH TOPPINGS

SKAGEN PRAWN SALAD

Toast skagen, or *skagenröra*, is named after the northern Danish town of Skagen. The dish was created by the Swedish chef Tore Wretman in the 1950s after a sailing trip along the Danish coast. Today, 'Toast skagen' is one of the most popular dishes in restaurants along the coast.

Serves 4

280g/10oz cooked peeled prawns
85g/3oz/6 tbsp mayonnaise (see page 90)
1 tbsp freshly squeezed lemon juice
4 slices of sourdough bread (see page 64)
4 tsp freshly grated horseradish

Pat the prawns dry on paper towels and chop roughly. Fold in the mayonnaise and lemon juice.

Toast the bread over an open fire or in a cast-iron pan. Serve with the prawns and freshly grated horseradish.

MUSHROOMS ON TOAST

Soaking the mushrooms in water for 5–10 minutes will clean them and will also prevent the mushrooms from absorbing more fat than necessary when sautéing them.

Serves 4

900g/2lb mixed mushrooms, such as chanterelles, porcini, portobello
4 tsp vegetable oil
1 shallot, sliced
2 tsp fennel seeds
225ml/8fl oz/scant 1 cup dry white wine
120ml/4fl oz/½ cup dry sherry
2 tsp salt
4 slices of sourdough bread (see page 64)
4 tsp extra virgin olive oil
2 tsp chopped fresh chives

Put the mushrooms in a large bowl and cover with plenty of cold water. Carefully lift the mushrooms out of the water, leaving any dirt at the bottom of the bowl, and drain on paper towels.

Heat a cast-iron pan over high heat. Add the vegetable oil and mushrooms, and sauté for 5 minutes, stirring constantly. Add the shallot and fennel seeds, and sauté for a further 3 minutes. Add the wine, sherry and salt. Bring to the boil and cook over high heat until all the liquid has evaporated.

Toast the bread over an open fire or in a cast-iron pan. Drizzle the olive oil over the toast and serve with the mushrooms, sprinkled with the chives.

EMBER-COOKED GRAVLAX WITH MUSTARD SAUCE AND SOURDOUGH TOAST

The gravlax takes 3 days to cure. You can eat it cold, but for a change I like to cook it briefly and serve it with toast.

Serves 4

350g/12oz skinless, boneless salmon loin, in one piece
40g/1½oz curing salt and sugar mix (see page 40)
4 slices of sourdough bread (see page 64)
4 tbsp mustard sauce (see page 96)
freshly ground black pepper

Rub the salmon with the curing mix and leave at room temperature for about 30 minutes until the sugar and salt have dissolved. Place in the refrigerator for 3 days, turning the fish over each day.

Start the fire with enough firewood to create a bed of embers.

Rinse the salmon briefly in cold water and dry with paper towels. Put the salmon in the embers and cook for about 2 minutes on each side. Place it on a chopping board and clean off the larger pieces of ash, then cut it diagonally into 2cm/¾in thick pieces.

Toast the bread over an open fire or in a cast-iron pan. Serve with the ember-cooked gravlax and mustard sauce, with freshly ground black pepper.

CHICKEN LIVER PÂTÉ WITH SOURDOUGH TOAST

A simple way of making pâté. Great as a starter with pickles, as well as for your breakfast sandwich.

Serves 4

Pink pickled onions
1 red onion, sliced
90ml/3fl oz/6 tbsp pickling liquid 1-2-3
   (see page 40), cooled

450g/1lb chicken livers
350g/12oz/1½ cups butter, at room temperature
4 tsp Calvados
2 shallots, finely chopped
½ apple, peeled and finely chopped
150ml/5fl oz/scant ⅔ cup dry white wine
1 tsp salt
4 slices of sourdough bread (see page 64)
4 tsp chopped fresh parsley

Combine the red onion and pickling liquid. Cover and store in a cold place for 4 hours.

Drain the chicken livers on paper towels for 30 minutes.

Heat a frying pan over high heat, add 30g/1oz of the butter, and sauté the livers until lightly coloured. Turn down the heat, add the Calvados, and cook until the livers are almost cooked through but still slightly pink in the centre (check by piercing a liver with a small sharp knife). Remove from the pan and set aside.

In the same pan, heat 30g/1oz of the butter and sauté the shallots and apple until soft but not coloured. Add the wine and simmer until reduced to about 5 tablespoons. Add the salt and chicken livers and bring to the boil. Place in a blender and blend until smooth. Add the remaining butter, a little at a time, and blend to a smooth paste. Place in a bowl or jar, cover and store in the refrigerator for 2 hours before serving.

Toast the bread over an open fire or in a cast-iron pan. Serve with chicken liver pâté, pickled red onion and chopped parsley.

BRUSCHETTA AND FRESH SOUR CREAM CHEESE

Even though the tomato season is short in Sweden, I always make sure I get my grilled tomato sandwich.

Serves 4

2 tomatoes
1 tsp salt
4 slices of sourdough bread (see page 64)
85g/3oz/6 tbsp fresh sour cream cheese
   (see page 61)
freshly ground black pepper
1 tbsp extra virgin olive oil

Cut the tomatoes in half and grill over medium–high heat on a grill grate over embers, starting with the cut surface down. Turn and cook with the skin side down until semi-dried. Season with salt.

Toast the bread over an open fire or in a cast-iron pan. Spread the toast with the fresh cheese, add half a grilled tomato, some black pepper and olive oil.

FRESH CHEESE, CHANTERELLES AND PICKLED RAMSON BUDS

It's a great adventure for me and my family to pick chanterelles at the end of the summer; it's like finding gold in the woods. If chanterelles are not in season you could use other mushrooms, sliced or quartered if large.

Serves 4

85g/3oz/6 tbsp butter
450g/1lb chanterelles, cleaned
1 shallot, quartered
55g/2oz/⅓ cup broad beans (fava beans),
   peeled and blanched
1 tsp finely chopped fresh parsley
salt
85g/3oz fresh sour cream cheese (see page 61)
4 tsp pickled ramson buds (see page 44)

Heat a cast-iron pan over high heat, add the butter and sauté the chanterelles for 2 minutes. Add the shallots, broad beans and parsley, and sauté for a further 2 minutes. Season with salt. Serve immediately, with fresh cheese and pickled ramson buds.

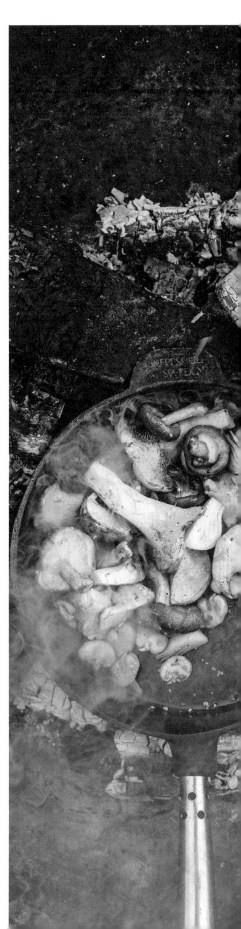

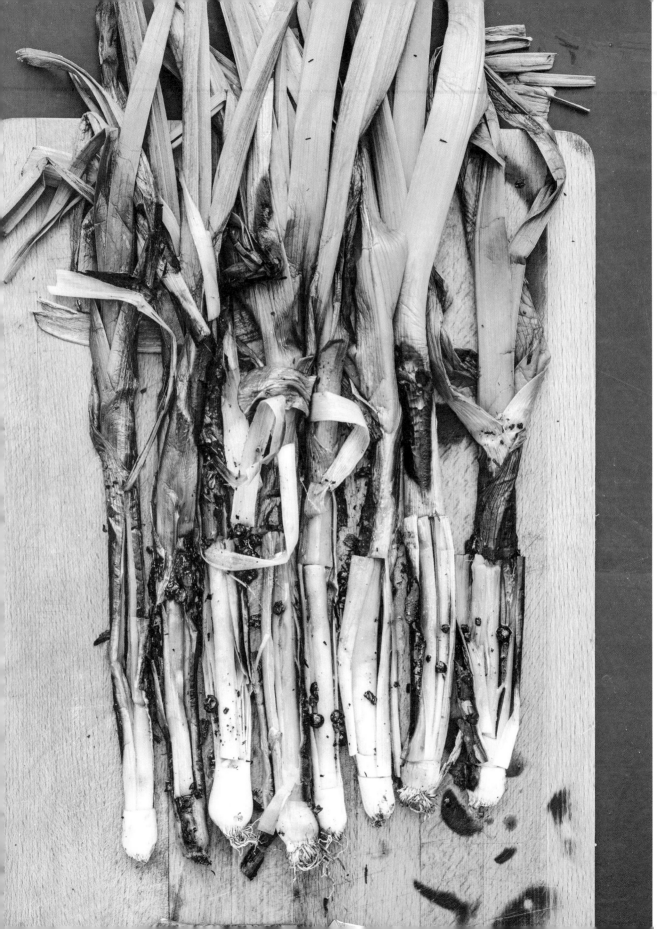

EMBER-BAKED LEEKS

If you can get really young, slim, fresh leeks, this recipe will be even better. Soaking the leeks in cold water will help them to cook without burning, but don't worry if the outer layer burns, as it will be peeled off. This is great as a starter or a side dish to meat or fish.

Serves 4

2 leeks or 4 large spring onions (scallions)
85g/3oz/6 tbsp homemade butter (see page 56),
    at room temperature
30g/1oz/2 tbsp rosé pepper salt (see page 36)

Start the fire, using enough firewood to create a bed of embers.

Keep the roots on the leeks. Clean the leeks in cold running water, then put them in a bowl, cover with cold water and leave for 20 minutes.

Pour off the water and dry the leeks with paper towels. Place the leeks in the embers and cook for about 6–8 minutes, turning once or twice, until tender all the way through.

Remove from the fire and peel off the burnt layers. Serve with homemade butter and rosé pepper salt.

GRILLED ARTICHOKES WITH JUNIPER BUTTER

A great starter you can make while preparing the main course on the same fire. You can precook the artichokes a day ahead, if wished.

Serves 4

2 globe artichokes, trimmed
½ lemon
6 tsp salt
55g/2oz/4 tbsp juniper butter (see page 56)

Start the fire, using firewood, and place a grill grate over it.

Put the artichokes in a pan, add the lemon and cover with water. Add the salt and bring to the boil over medium–high heat. Simmer for about 30 minutes or until a leaf pulls out easily. Drain the artichokes and leave them upside down to drain and cool.

Cut the artichokes in half and remove the chokes. Grill the artichokes, cut side down, over medium heat on the grill grate for 5–8 minutes until lightly charred. Serve hot, with juniper butter.

STUFFED EGGS WITH PRAWNS AND HAY SALT

Stuffed eggs are a great dish for brunch or at the *smörgåsbord*. In Sweden the eggs are traditionally topped with mayonnaise and prawns, or whipped cream and a paste of smoked cod roe, potatoes and tomato paste (sold in tubes under the brand name Kalles Kaviar). This recipe is inspired by American devilled eggs.

Serves 4

6 eggs
85g/3oz/6 tbsp mayonnaise (see below)
2 tbsp sour cream
1 tsp Dijon mustard
¼ tsp Tabasco sauce
salt
280g/10oz cooked peeled prawns
1 tbsp freshly grated horseradish
1 tsp finely chopped fresh dill
1 tsp hay salt (see page 36)
1 lemon, cut into eight wedges

Mayonnaise
2 egg yolks
1 tsp Dijon mustard
1 tsp salt
350ml/12fl oz/1½ cups vegetable oil
2 tsp freshly squeezed lemon juice

First, make the mayonnaise. Put the egg yolks into a wide bowl and add the mustard and salt. Using a balloon whisk, beat until pale and creamy. Keep whisking and pour in the oil a few drops at a time until the mixture emulsifies and thickens. Add the lemon juice.

Put the eggs in a saucepan and cover with cold water. Bring to the boil and cook for 10 minutes. Cool in iced water, then peel off the shells. Cut the eggs in half lengthways and scoop the yolks into a bowl.

Mix the egg yolks, mayonnaise, sour cream, mustard and Tabasco, and season with salt to taste. Pipe the egg yolk mixture on top of the egg whites. Top with the prawns and grated horseradish, then sprinkle with chopped dill and hay salt. Serve with lemon wedges.

ON SMÖRGÅSBORD

The Swedish term *smörgåsbord* consists of the words *smörgås* (meaning 'open-faced sandwich') and *bord* (meaning 'table'). Originally, *smörgåsbord* was something that was served as a snack, together with spirits. It could be a simple starter, with cold cuts of meat or pickled fish. Today, the *smörgåsbord* has developed and has taken several turns within Swedish gastronomy. At the beginning of the twentieth century, in 1912 to be precise, when Stockholm hosted the Olympic Games, local restaurants took the opportunity to serve Swedish delicacies to the visitors. It was the starting point of the international launch of the *smörgåsbord* concept. In the US, it was adopted immediately and remains well established to this day. There, it developed into a buffet spread and, quite shortly afterwards, that also became the norm in Sweden.

In the 1960s, the famous Swedish chef of the time, Tore Wretman, decided to reintroduce the *smörgåsbord* to fine-dining salons and started to serve *smörgåsbord* at the prestigious Operakällaren, in Stockholm. Tore's updated *smörgåsbord* quickly became a success and people travelled from all over the country to sample it. Nowadays, Swedes don't eat *smörgåsbord* in the same sense, rather it has developed into the buffet we eat at Christmas. Gradually, however, the Swedish *smörgåsbord* is once again enjoying a renaissance, this time in the form of a selection of small tapas dishes. Making homemade pickled fish, charcuteries and the Christmas buffet speciality, *lutfisk* (a dried cod dish that has been treated with lye), has become incredibly popular. Old techniques are being rediscovered, and it is the continuing popularity of both the Christmas buffet and the *smörgåsbord* that has strongly contributed to the fact that Swedish cooks have been able to retain old food-preparation techniques and skills.

'SOS' PICKLED HERRING 3 WAYS WITH HAY-SALTED BOILED POTATOES

Sill Ost Smör (SOS), literally means herring cheese butter. Herring is Sweden's most important fish, together with salmon. We preserve it in many different ways – pickled, cured, smoked, fermented – and it is a major part of a *smörgåsbord. Hovmästarsås* mustard sauce is usually made with dill and served with gravlax but is also great used here to cure the herring.

We have two different kinds of herring. That from the south of the island of Öland on the west coast of Sweden is called *sill* (the general term for herring); this saltwater fish is larger and fattier than the freshwater Baltic herring, or *strömming*. The northern Baltic Sea has very low salinity because of the hundreds of rivers that flow into it, and many freshwater fish live there. The infamous delicacy *surströmming*, or Swedish fermented herring, is most common along the Baltic coast.

Serves 4

Juniper pickled herring
2 fillets of salted herring
½ red onion, thinly sliced
1 clove
1 allspice berry
6 juniper berries, crushed
450ml/16fl oz/2 cups pickling liquid 1-2-3
    (see page 40), cooled

Mustard sauce 'hovmästarsås'
85g/3oz/6 tbsp mild mustard
30g/1oz/2 tbsp caster (superfine) sugar
175ml/6fl oz/¾ cup rapeseed oil
1 tbsp *ättika* (Swedish white vinegar), or 2 tbsp white
    wine vinegar (you may need to add a little more oil
    for a thicker consistency)

Mustard herring
450ml/16fl oz/2 cups water
4 tsp caster (superfine) sugar
5 tsp salt
250g/9oz fresh herring fillets, skinned

Blackened herring
2 large fresh herrings, about 25cm/10in long,
    gutted, fins trimmed off
salt
30g/1oz/3 tbsp chopped leek
30g/1oz/3 tbsp chopped red onion
2 cloves
1 allspice berry
1 bay leaf
900ml/32fl oz/3¾ cups pickling liquid 1-2-3
    (see page 40), cooled

Hay-salted boiled potatoes
900g/2lb new potatoes
55g/2oz/3 tbsp hay salt
    (see page 36)
1 bunch of dill

To make the juniper pickled herring, put the herring fillets in a large bowl, cover with water and store in the refrigerator for 12 hours. Drain the fish and trim off any fins. Cut the herring into 2cm/¾in pieces and place in a sterilized jar with the onion and spices. Cover with pickling liquid and store in a cold place for 3 days.

To make the mustard sauce, mix the mustard and sugar in a bowl and beat with an electric whisk until the sugar has dissolved. Keep whisking and pour in the oil a few drops at a time, until the mixture thickens and emulsifies. Add the vinegar.

To make the mustard herring, mix the water, sugar and salt in a bowl. Add the herring fillets and store in the refrigerator for 12–16 hours. To check if the herring is cured enough, break open the thickest

part of a fillet: if it is grey or slightly pink it is
ready. Drain off as much liquid as possible and dry
on paper towels. Fold into the mustard sauce and
store in a cold place for 2 days.

To make the blackened herring: start the fire with
birch firewood and burn down until you get a solid
glow over the entire surface of the firewood. If
you don't want to use open fire, use a really hot
cast-iron pan.

Clean the herrings inside and out, rinse in cold
water, dry with paper towels and season with salt.

Turn a glowing surface of the firewood face-up and
place the herrings on top. Cook for 3–4 minutes
on both sides. You may need to do this in batches.
Remove from the wood and carefully place on a
tray or plate. Leave in the refrigerator to cool for
about 1 hour.

Cut off the heads. Place the blackened herrings in
a sterilized jar, add the leek, onion and spices, and
cover with pickling liquid. Store in the refrigerator
for 2 days.

Put the potatoes, hay salt and dill in a saucepan and
add water to barely cover. Cover with a lid, bring
to the boil over high heat and simmer for about
3 minutes. Turn off the heat and leave in the pan
for 15 minutes. Test with a stick (or skewer): the
potatoes should be tender in the middle. If not,
bring back to the boil, remove from the heat and
leave for a further 5 minutes. Test again and repeat
if necessary. Drain and leave in the pan with the lid
off until the steam disappears.

Serve one, two or three types of herring with the
burned hay potatoes, crispbread (see page 68) and
homemade butter (see page 56) and some mature
cheese or *potkäs* (see page 62), with lager beer and
Swedish *snaps* (aquavit).

EMBER-COOKED HERRING IN NEWSPAPER WITH CRISPBREAD AND LINGONBERRIES

This old-fashioned cooking technique works for many kinds of fish – try trout, mackerel, or even a larger fish such as a 2–2.5kg/ about 4–6lb salmon – as well as for potatoes and root vegetables. If you can't find frozen lingonberries, you could serve the herring with preserved redcurrants (see page 48) or pickled gooseberries (see page 46).

Serves 4

350g/12oz/3½ cups frozen lingonberries
115g/4oz/generous ½ cup caster (superfine) sugar
4 large or 12 small Baltic fresh herrings, gutted
salt
4 pieces of crispbread (see page 68)
115g/4oz/½ cup juniper butter (see page 56),
   melted

Put the lingonberries and sugar in a large bowl, stir until the sugar has dissolved, then set aside at room temperature for 1–2 hours.

Start the fire with birch firewood.

Clean the herrings inside and out, dry with paper towels and season with salt. Wrap each herring in a double layer of newspaper, making a parcel, then soak the newspaper in water for a few minutes. Place the parcels in the embers and cook for 25–40 minutes until the paper starts to burn.

Open the parcels (the fish skin will peel off with the newspaper) and serve the herring on crispbread, with the lingonberries and melted juniper butter.

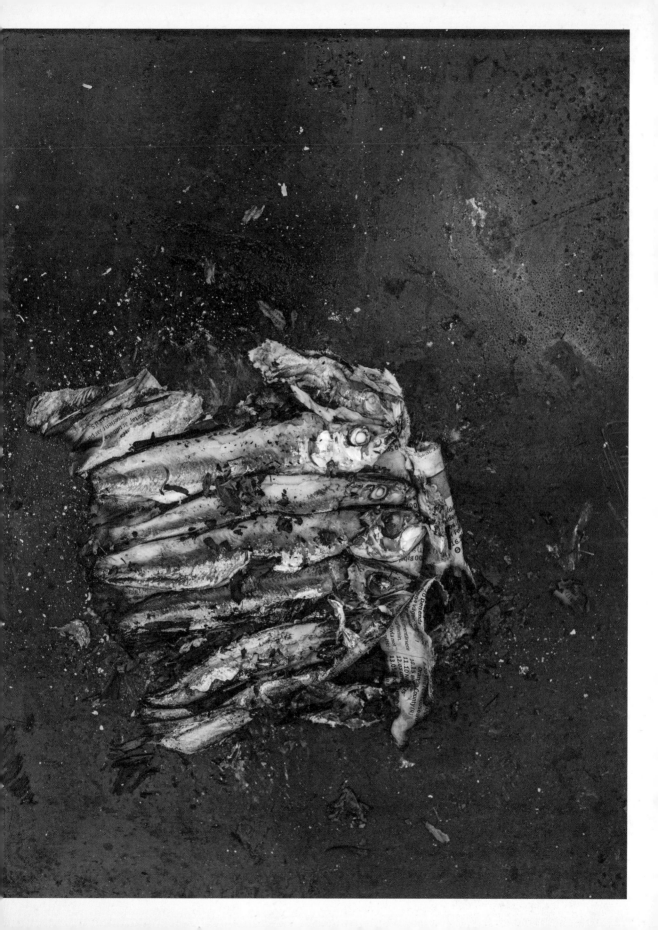

SMOKED VENDACE ROE WITH HOMEMADE SOUR CREAM AND CURED LEMON ON FLATBREAD

Vendace is a small fish found in northern European lakes and in the northern Baltic Sea. Its roe is a deep orange colour and is considered a delicacy, often served at Nobel Prize banquets. Salmon roe (salmon caviar) is larger, but could be used in this recipe. You will need to start 2 days in advance to make the sour cream.

Alder wood chips are ideal for your smoker, or a branch of juniper.

Serves 4

225ml/8fl oz/scant 1 cup double (heavy) cream
1 tbsp buttermilk, or use the whey from making
    butter (see page 56)
½ lemon, cut into 4 wedges
1 tsp curing salt and sugar mix (see page 40)
200g/7oz vendace roe
½ red onion, finely chopped
4 pieces of flatbread (see page 70)
sprigs of dill

Combine the cream and buttermilk in a bowl. Cover and leave to stand at room temperature for 2 days. Store the homemade sour cream in the refrigerator for up to 5 days.

Combine the lemon wedges with the curing mix and leave in the refrigerator for 12 hours. Pour off the liquid and chop the lemon into small pieces.

Prepare a smoker. Place a handful of wood chips, or the juniper branch, in a 15cm-/5 in-high saucepan with a lid. Alternatively, use a wide tin can with the top removed. Place over a high heat on the stove or over your open fire and leave until smoky. Remove from the heat.

Spread the roe on a metal tray, refrigerate until cold, then place in the smoker for 3–5 minutes. It should not be cooked, just lightly smoked. Alternatively, place the roe in a fine sieve and place above the smoke and cover. Smoke for 3–5 minutes, as above.

Remove from the smoker and place the tray, or sieve, of roe on a bed of ice to cool down. Taste, and if it needs to be smokier, put it back in the smoker for another 3–5 minutes.

Serve the smoked roe, sour cream and chopped red onion on flatbread, sprinkled with dill, and pieces of lemon.

HOTDOGS WITH TOPPINGS

A great idea for a picnic. Give your friends a selection of toppings to eat with traditional grilled hotdogs.

Serves 4

4 frankfurter sausages
4 hotdog rolls, sliced in half
creamy potato and caper salad (see below)
prawn salad (see page 74), sprinkled with
   1 tbsp chopped fresh parsley
sautéed mushrooms (see page 74)
2 tsp chopped fresh chives
pink pickled onions (see page 81)

Creamy potato and caper salad
225g/8oz cold cooked potatoes
3 tbsp mayonnaise (see page 90)
30g/1oz capers
1 tsp red wine vinegar

To make the potato and caper salad: cut the potatoes into roughly 1cm/½in cubes. Place in a serving bowl and fold in the mayonnaise, capers and vinegar. Chill until ready to serve.

Make the prawn salad and chill until ready to serve, then sprinkle with parsley.

The mushrooms can be cleaned up to an hour in advance. Cook them in a cast-iron pan – over the picnic fire, if you like – just before serving, and sprinkle with chives.

Grill the sausages over an open fire. Serve in the rolls, with the toppings on the side for everyone to help themselves.

JUNIPER-SMOKED SALMON AND HOMEMADE SOUR CREAM

The salmon will need 3 days to cure before smoking. Here, it is served warm with crispbread, but you can also add it to a flatbread base for a Swedish 'pizza' (see recipe overleaf). Once smoked, you can leave the salmon to cool, then store in the refrigerator for 2–3 days.

Serves 4

450g/1lb salmon loin
30g/1oz curing salt and sugar mix (see page 40)
6 juniper stems
4 pieces of crispbread (see page 68)
150ml/5fl oz/scant ⅔ cup homemade sour cream (see page 104)
6 tsp freshly grated horseradish

Rub the salmon with the curing mix. Leave at room temperature for 30 minutes until the sugar and salt have dissolved, then store in the refrigerator for 3 days. Turn once a day.

To smoke the salmon, first soak the juniper stems in water for 10 minutes. Start the fire with birch firewood. Dry the salmon with paper towels. Place the juniper on the fire and place the salmon on top. Let it coook in the smoke and steam for 5–8 minutes or until the stems catch fire.

Remove the salmon, slice and serve with crispbread, sour cream and grated horseradish.

FLATBREAD WITH SMOKED SALMON, ONIONS, HOMEMADE SOUR CREAM AND ROCKET

My interpretation of a Swedish pizza. Try this with other toppings, such as cured venison, mayonnaise and freshly grated horseradish.

Makes 8 pizzas

700g/1½lb juniper-smoked salmon (double the recipe on page 110), thinly sliced (alternatively use store-bought cold-smoked salmon)
120ml/4fl oz/½ cup homemade sour cream (see page 104)
55g/2oz pink pickled onions (see page 81)
1 bunch of rocket
freshly ground black pepper

Pizza dough
40g/1½oz/2 cakes fresh yeast
300ml/10fl oz/1¼ cups lukewarm water
350g/12oz/scant 3 cups strong white bread flour, plus extra for dusting
1 tsp salt
3 tbsp olive oil
2 tsp sugar

To make the pizza dough: mix the yeast with the water until dissolved, and set aside for 5–10 minutes. Sift the flour and salt into a food processor or a large bowl. Add the yeast liquid, olive oil, and sugar. Mix to form a dough and knead – in the processor or by hand – until the dough is smooth and springy. Place the ball of dough in a large, flour-dusted bowl and flour the top of it. Cover the bowl with a damp tea towel and leave in a warm place for about 1 hour until the dough has doubled in size.

Preheat the oven to 200°C/400°F/gas 6. Lightly flour a large baking sheet.

Turn out the dough onto a floured work surface, then divide it into eight equal pieces. Roll out each piece with a rolling pin, or stretch by hand, to about 5mm/¼in thick and place on the floured baking sheet. Working in batches (depending on the size of your baking sheet), cook each pizza for about 3 minutes. It should be baked all the way through, but not coloured. Remove from the oven and leave to cool on a wire rack, covering the pizza with a tea towel.

To serve: grill the pizzas on a grill grate over an open fire, or cook them in a large, hot, cast-iron pan for about 3 minutes on each side until lightly browned.

Top with smoked salmon, sour cream, pickled onion, rocket and black pepper, and serve at once.

JUNIPER-SMOKED TURBOT, ROASTED ONION AND BROWN BUTTER MAYONNAISE

I find brown butter harmonizes with smoky flavours and I use it a lot.

Serves 4

1 tbsp green juniper berries
1 tsp salt
55g/2oz/4 tbsp butter
450g/1lb turbot fillet
1 juniper stem

Brown butter mayonnaise
2 egg yolks
1 tsp Dijon mustard
1 tsp salt
175ml/6fl oz/¾ cup vegetable oil
175g/6oz/¾ cup brown butter (see page 58),
    melted and cooled slightly
1 tbsp sherry vinegar

Cast-iron roasted onions
4 mild onions
1 tbsp vegetable oil
2 garlic cloves, peeled
3 sprigs of thyme
85g/3oz/6 tbsp butter
1 tsp salt

To make the brown butter mayonnaise: put the egg yolks in a wide bowl and add the mustard and salt. Using a balloon whisk, beat until pale and creamy. Keep whisking and pour in the oil a few drops at a time until the mixture emulsifies. Whisk in the brown butter in the same way; if it gets too thick, add a few drops of cold water. Finally, whisk in the vinegar. Chill until ready to serve.

For the roasted onions, preheat the oven to 200°C/400°F/gas 6. Peel the onions, keeping as much as possible of the root. Put the onions, roots downward, on a chopping board and make three cuts from the top down to the root – without cutting all the way through the root. Each onion should now have six wedges held together by the root. Heat a cast-iron pan over medium–high heat. Add the onions, oil, garlic and thyme, and mix well, without breaking up the onions. Put the pan in the oven and cook for about 15–20 minutes, until the onion is golden brown and slightly burned on the top. Add the butter and salt, cover with a lid and cook for about 20 minutes until the onions are soft all the way through: test by pressing a small knife into the centre of an onion. Remove from the oven, strain off and reserve the liquid.

For the turbot, preheat the oven to 120°C/250°F/gas ½. Grind the juniper berries and salt in a mortar, then mix with the butter. Dry the turbot with a paper towel and rub the butter over the fish on both sides. Put the fish in a deep roasting pan or baking tray with sides about 20cm/8in high and a surface three times larger than the fish. Place the juniper stem to the side of the fish. If the roasting pan doesn't have a lid, make a lid out of foil to cover it; keep on one side. Put the pan in the oven and bake for about 20 minutes or until the internal temperature of the fish reaches 46°C/115°F. If you don't have a cooking thermometer, make a cut in the thickest part of the fish: it should be white and cooked all the way through.

Remove from the oven and turn off the heat. Set the juniper on fire and let it burn for 10 seconds. Cover with the lid, making sure the fire is out. Put the pan back in the oven and leave to smoke for 10 minutes.

Cut the smoked turbot into four pieces, brush with the juice from roasting the onions, and serve with the roasted onions and brown butter mayonnaise.

CURED VENISON, LEEK ASH, PORCINI CRÈME, BLACKCURRANT VINAIGRETTE AND RYE BREAD CRISPS

Herds of reindeer are kept in many parts of northern Sweden. I use this simple cure to showcase the flavour of the meat; any type of venison loin benefits from this treatment. You will need to cure the venison for 3 days before serving.

Serves 4

280g/10oz boneless venison loin
4 tsp curing salt and sugar mix (see page 40)
¼ leek
porcini crème (see below)
blackcurrant vinaigrette (see below)
¼ loaf of rye bread (see page 67)
1 bunch of micro salad leaves

Porcini crème
450g/1lb porcini mushrooms, cleaned
900ml/32fl oz/3¾ cups vegetable oil
1 shallot, sliced
1 garlic clove, sliced
40g/1½oz/3 tbsp butter
salt and freshly ground black pepper

Blackcurrant vinaigrette
1 tbsp vegetable oil
1 shallot, finely chopped
2 tbsp blackcurrant vinegar, or sherry vinegar
55g/2oz/½ cup blackcurrants, cleaned
90ml/3fl oz/6 tbsp rapeseed oil

Rub the venison with the curing mix. Leave at room temperature for 30 minutes until the sugar and salt have dissolved, then store in a plastic bag in the refrigerator for 3 days. Turn once a day.

To make the porcini crème, put the porcini in a saucepan with the oil. Cook at 95°C/200°F (just below boiling point) for 2 hours. Strain off the oil. Sauté the shallot, garlic and porcini for 2–3 minutes. Using a blender, blend the porcini mixture with the butter until smooth. Season with salt and pepper to taste.

To make the blackcurrant vinaigrette, heat the vegetable oil in a pan over medium heat and sauté the shallot for 2–3 minutes. Add the vinegar and boil until reduced by half. Add the blackcurrants and simmer for 3 minutes. Remove from the heat and add the rapeseed oil. Season with salt to taste and leave to cool.

Preheat the oven to 250°C/480°F/gas 10. Clean the leek in cold water. Drain and separate the layers and spread them on a baking tray. Bake in the oven until totally black. Remove from the oven and turn the oven down to 120°C/250°F/gas ½. Crush the burned leek to an ash powder.

Slice the rye bread thinly, place on a baking sheet and dry in the oven for about 20 minutes.

Dry the venison with paper towels and roll in the leek ash. Cut thinly on the diagonal and place on four plates. Top with porcini crème, rye bread crackers, blackcurrant vinaigrette and micro salad leaves.

CRUSHED NEW POTATOES, TRUFFLE AND POACHED CAST-IRON ROASTED ONION

Simple and delicious. The flavour of the truffle is highlighted by the butteriness of the potatoes and the sweetness from the onions.

Serves 4

175g/6oz/¾ cup butter
700g/1½lb new potatoes, scrubbed
1 fresh black truffle, about 15g/½oz
1 tsp chopped fresh chives

Poached cast-iron roasted onions
4 mild onions
1 tbsp vegetable oil
2 garlic cloves, peeled
3 sprigs of thyme
85g/3oz butter
1 tsp salt
450ml/16fl oz/2 cups chicken stock

To make the roasted onions, preheat the oven to 200°C/400°F/gas 6. Peel the onions, keeping as much as possible of the root. Put the onions, roots downward, on a chopping board and make three cuts from the top down to the root – without cutting all the way through the root. Each onion should now have six wedges held together by the root. Heat a cast-iron pan over medium–high heat. Add the onions, oil, garlic and thyme, and mix well, without breaking up the onions. Put the pan in the oven and cook for about 15–20 minutes, until the onion is golden brown and slightly burned on the top. Add the butter, salt and chicken stock, cover with a lid and cook for about 20 minutes until the onions are soft all the way through: test by pressing a small knife into the centre of an onion. Remove from the oven and leave to cool slightly, then strain off and reserve the liquid.

Turn the oven down to 180°C/350°F/gas 4. Rub half the butter over the potatoes and spread out on a baking tray. Bake in the oven for about 25 minutes. Gently crush the potatoes without breaking them up.

Put 90ml/3fl oz/6 tablespoons of the liquid from the poached roasted onions in a saucepan over a low heat, add the remaining butter and, using a hand-held blender, blend until foamy.

Serve the potatoes and a poached roasted onion on four plates. Top with some foam, chopped chives and freshly grated truffle, and serve at once.

SEAWEED-STEAMED SCALLOP, WITH SEARED CUCUMBER AND LIME

You may be able to order seaweed from your local fish market. Alternatively, if you spend a day at the seaside you can pick it yourself. Make sure you cut living seaweed direct from the rocks it grows on. It's not advisable to collect washed-up seaweed from the shore.

Serves 4

½ cucumber, peeled
4 fresh scallops in their shells, cleaned, reserving the roes and the bottom shells
55g/2oz/4 tbsp butter
2.25kg/5lb wrack (or another large seaweed)
pinch salt, to season
1 lime, cut into wedges

Start the fire with birch firewood and keep it burning. It should be about 60cm/2ft wide.

Cut the cucumber on the diagonal into 3cm/1¼in pieces and sear on both sides in a dry cast-iron pan over high heat. Remove the cucumber and set aside.

In the cast-iron pan, sear the scallops on both sides over high heat for about 2 minutes. Remove the pan from the heat and remove the scallops from the pan. Add butter to the pan and set aside.

Ensure the fire is strong, and put the seaweed on the fire. Quickly place the cucumber, roes and scallops on top of the seaweed. Let it steam and smoke for 5–8 minutes or until the seaweed almost catches fire.

Transfer the scallops and cucumber to the scallop shells. Heat the butter in the pan until it foams, then pour into the shells. Season with salt and serve at once, with a wedge of lime on the side.

FLAMED OYSTERS WITH SHALLOT AND APPLE DRESSING

I love raw oysters, served only with fresh lemon juice, but sometimes it is fun to try something new, and this is certainly an exciting way to serve them. This uses the *flambadou* cooking technique (see page 32 for more information; for suppliers see page 237).

Serves 4

2 shallots, peeled and finely chopped
½ apple, peeled and finely chopped
4 tbsp sherry vinegar
1 tsp chopped fennel fronds or dill
12 oysters
55g/2oz/4 tbsp beef tallow, cleaned, cut
    into 2cm/¾in cubes, at room temperature
    (alternatively, beef dripping could be substituted)
450g/1lb/1½ cups salt, to serve

Fill the *flambadou* with glowing embers and place in an open fire.

Combine the shallots, apple, vinegar and fennel or dill in a bowl and set aside.

Open the oysters and place on a stable fire-resistant surface.

Take the *flambadou* out of the fire and pour out the embers. It should be red hot. Carefully place some of the tallow in the *flambadou* and quickly turn it over the flames so it catches fire. Hold the *flambadou* over the oysters and drip the hot fat over the oysters, for about 5 seconds on each oyster. Repeat the process to cook all the oysters.

Alternative method: heat a small cast iron pan over a very high heat. Wearing heat-proof oven gloves to protect your hands and arms, carefully place the tallow (or beef dripping) in the hot pan and quickly turn it into a flame to ignite the fat. Hold the pan over the oysters and drip the hot, flaming fat over.

Add about 4 tsp water to the salt and mix to a white paste – this makes it more stable as a base for the oyster shells. Form the salt into 12 rough piles and place an oyster on top of each pile. Top the oysters with a little of the shallot and apple dressing.

SEARED LANGOUSTINE, KOHLRABI AND SMOKED BUTTER

It is important not to overcook the langoustines. Sear them quickly over very high heat, on one side only; they will continue cooking after they are removed from the heat.

Serves 4

4 langoustines
salt
2 tsp vegetable oil
175g/6oz kohlrabi
30g/1oz/2 tbsp smoked butter (see page 58)
a few edible flowers

Langoustine sauce
900g/2lb chicken bones
2 shallots, peeled and halved
1 garlic clove
1 sprig of thyme
55g/2oz/4 tbsp unsalted butter
2 tsp sherry vinegar

To make the langoustine sauce, put the chicken bones, shallots, garlic and thyme in a saucepan and add water to cover. Bring to the boil, then reduce the heat and simmer for 6 hours.

Remove the langoustines from their shells and set the langoustines aside until needed. Add the langoustine shells to the pan with the chicken bones and simmer for a further 1 hour. Remove from the heat and leave to stand for 1–2 hours. Strain through cheesecloth and leave to cool completely.

Skim off the fat from the surface of the stock, then boil until reduced and well flavoured. Remove from the heat, whisk in the butter and sherry vinegar, and season with salt to taste.

Cut the kohlrabi into thin, noodle-like strips. Bring a saucepan of salted water to the boil, add the kohlrabi and cook for 3 minutes. Drain and cool in iced water. Drain well and set aside.

Heat a cast-iron pan until very hot. Thread the langoustines onto skewers. Season with salt, brush with oil and sear on one side in the hot pan. Place the langoustines, seared side up, on a metal tray and leave to finish cooking to perfection. If they need to cook longer, finish in the oven at 80°C/175°F (the lowest possible setting). Remove from the skewers.

Put the cooked kohlrabi and smoked butter in a saucepan over medium heat to heat through. Serve with the seared langoustine and sauce, with edible flowers.

STEAK TARTARE WITH ONION RINGS

Serve a buffet of meat and accompaniments, not forgetting sea salt and a pepper mill. Let your guests create their own steak tartare.

Serves 4

700g/1½lb fillet (tenderloin), or another tender, good-quality steak
3 tsp rowan capers (see page 136), or regular capers
3 tsp Dijon mustard
4 tsp cold-pressed rapeseed oil
4 tsp freshly grated horseradish
175g/6oz mixed salad leaves
sea salt and freshly ground black pepper

Deep-fried onion rings

2 onions, peeled
450ml/16fl oz/2 cups milk
oil for deep-frying
55g/2oz/½ cup flour
salt

Cut meat into pieces about 3 x 4cm/about 1½in, then either grind coarsely in a mincer, or cut the meat into 5mm/¼in cubes. Cover and store in a cool place while you make the onion rings.

To make the onion rings: using a mandolin, slice the onions into thin rings. Try to keep the layers together, then remove the centre part of the onions. Place in a bowl, add the milk and leave to soak for 1 hour.

Pour off the milk and drain the onion rings on paper towels. Heat the oil in a deep-fat fryer or large saucepan to 180°C/350°F; if you don't have a cooking thermometer, drop a cube of bread into the oil – if bubbles immediately form around the bread, the oil is hot enough.

Sprinkle the flour over the onion rings and toss well to ensure all the onion is coated with flour. Deep-fry until golden brown. Drain on paper towels and season with salt.

In separate bowls, serve the meat, capers, mustard, rapeseed oil, horseradish, onion rings, salad leaves, salt and pepper. You could also serve with crispbread (see page 68) or hay-salted boiled potatoes (see page 96).

CARAMELIZED WALNUT, APPLE
AND WATERCRESS SALAD

Serve as a starter or as a snack with vegetable sticks to dip into the blue cheese sauce.

Serves 4

150g/5oz blue cheese
90ml/3fl oz/6 tbsp milk
1 Granny Smith or other tart apple
2 bunches of watercress, cleaned,
    large stems removed

Caramelized walnuts
225g/8oz/1 cup sugar
225ml/8fl oz/scant 1 cup water
225g/8oz/scant 2 cups walnuts
oil for deep-frying

To make the caramelized walnuts, put the sugar and water in a saucepan over medium–high heat and bring to the boil until the sugar has dissolved. Add the walnuts and simmer for 1 minute. Lift out the walnuts with a slotted spoon and drain them on a tray, keeping them separate. Repeat the process twice more, using the same syrup.

Heat the oil in a deep-fat fryer or large saucepan to 180°C/350°F; if you don't have a cooking thermometer, drop a cube of bread into the oil – if bubbles immediately form around the bread, the oil is hot enough. Add the walnuts and fry for 3 minutes; they are ready when they float to the surface. Drain the deep-fried caramelized walnuts on a tray.

Combine the blue cheese and milk in a food processor and blend to a smooth dressing, adding more milk if necessary.

Slice the apple thinly, using a mandolin or knife. Place the watercress on a serving plate. Top with freshly sliced apple and lightly crushed caramelized walnuts and ripple the blue cheese dressing over the top.

BUTTERNUT SQUASH, FRESH CHEESE, KALE CRISPS AND ROWAN CAPERS

If you pick rowanberries in the autumn, you can preserve them with vinegar and sugar as rowan capers. But if you've missed the rowanberry season, regular capers work well, too. Make them at least a week before you embark on this salad. Pumpkin or sweet potato works equally well in this salad, in place of the squash.

Serves 4

8 large kale leaves
4 tbsp extra virgin olive oil
1½ tsp salt
1 butternut squash, peeled and deseeded
200g/7oz/generous ¾ cup spicy fresh cheese (see page 62), or ricotta
4 tsp rowan capers – alternatively use elderberry capers or regular capers

Rowan capers
450g/1lb/4½ cups freshly picked red rowanberries
450g/1lb/1½ cups salt
450ml/16fl oz/2 cups *ättika* (Swedish white vinegar), or 900ml/32fl oz/3¾ cups white wine vinegar
900g/2lb/5 cups sugar
900ml/32fl oz/3¾ cups water

To make the rowan capers, remove all the stalks and rinse the berries in cold water. Put the berries in a large pan and add the salt and water to cover. Bring to the boil and simmer for 5 minutes. Drain the berries and rinse in cold water.

Combine the vinegar, sugar and water in a large pan and heat until the sugar has dissolved. Add the berries and bring slowly to the boil over medium heat. Pour into a sterilized jar, cover with a lid and leave to cool.

Store in the refrigerator for a week before serving. They will keep for up to 1 year.

Preheat the oven to 200°C/400°F/gas 6. Clean the kale in cold water and dry with paper towels. Cut the kale into pieces about 5cm/2in square, place on a baking sheet and toss with 1 tablespoon of the olive oil and ½ teaspoon salt. Bake for 10–12 minutes until crisp.

Turn the oven down to 180°C/350°F/gas 4. Cut the butternut squash into roughly 2cm/¾in cubes and place on a baking sheet. Sprinkle with 2 tablespoons of olive oil and 1 teaspoon salt. Bake for about 25 minutes; use a knife to check that the squash is soft in the centre.

Serve the baked squash, kale crisps, fresh cheese and capers in a bowl. Sprinkle with 4 teaspoons of extra virgin olive oil and 4 teaspoons of pickling liquid from the rowan capers.

SAUTÉED CHANTERELLES, APPLE AND THYME

This is a great starter or a side dish for grilled beef (see page 144).

Serves 4

55g/2oz/4 tbsp butter
900g/2lb chanterelles, cleaned and cut into
   even-sized pieces
2 tsp salt
2 tsp fresh thyme leaves
2 tsp pickling liquid 1-2-3 (see page 40)
1 tart apple, sliced

Heat a cast-iron pan over high heat. Add the butter and chanterelles, and sauté for about 3–4 minutes, stirring frequently, until lightly golden brown.

Add the salt, thyme and pickling liquid and cook for 1 minute.

Serve at once, with freshly sliced apple.

CUCUMBER, STRAWBERRY AND PICKLED ELDERBERRY SALAD

A very simple, fresh summer salad, using cucumber from the greenhouse, strawberries from the garden and preserved elderberries from the trees in my neighbourhood. Great as a starter or a side dish with grilled fish.

Serves 4

1 cucumber, sliced
450g/1lb/3 cups strawberries, sliced
16 small bunches of pickled elderberries
   (see page 50)
2 tbsp cold-pressed rapeseed oil
salt
leaves from a bunch of fresh mint

Combine the cucumber and strawberries in a bowl. Add 2 tablespoons of the elderberry pickling liquid and the rapeseed oil and toss gently. Season with salt to taste.

Top with fresh mint leaves and serve the pickled elderberries scattered over the top.

BAKED CELERIAC, CAULIFLOWER, SMOKED BUTTER AND NASTURTIUM FLOWERS

Edible flowers are a great complement to this salad: beautiful and tasty.

Serves 4

1 small celeriac (celery root)
55g/2oz/4 tbsp butter
2 tbsp salt
12–16 nasturtium flowers
1 small cauliflower
2 tbsp pickling liquid 1-2-3 (see page 40)
85g/3oz smoked butter (see page 58), melted
2 tbsp sea salt
2 tbsp freshly grated horseradish
small sprigs of dill

Preheat the oven to 220°C/425°F/gas 7.

Clean the celeriac in cold water, scrub thoroughly and dry with paper towels. Rub with the butter and 1 tablespoon of salt, place in a baking tray and bake in the oven for 10 minutes. Turn the oven down to 180°C/350°F/gas 4 and bake for a further 40–60 minutes, until it is soft in the middle.

Put the nasturtium flowers in a bowl, cover with cold water and leave for 5 minutes. Drain and leave to dry on paper towels.

Clean the cauliflower in cold water and peel off the outer leaves. Cut the cauliflower into four equal parts, held together by the stalk. Bring a large saucepan of water to the boil, add 1 tablespoon of salt and add the cauliflower; boil gently until tender.

Cut the celeriac into wedges. Toss the flowers in the pickling liquid and serve with the cauliflower, celeriac, smoked butter, sea salt, grated horseradish and dill.

LARGE
DISHES

GRILLED BEEF, FLAVOURED SALT, BROWN BUTTER EMULSION AND MIXED SALAD

The best way to cook beef is on the bone, which keeps it tender and succulent. If possible, use grass-fed beef.

Serves 4

1.3kg/3lb beef on the bone
55g/2oz/3 tbsp sea salt
1 bunch of fresh radishes
1 red onion
1 fennel bulb
450g/1lb mixed salad leaves
juice of 1 lemon
3 tbsp olive oil
6 tsp flavoured salt (see recipes on page 36, or all three of them)

Brown butter emulsion

2 eggs
4 tsp sherry vinegar
2 tsp salt
175ml/6fl oz/¾ cup vegetable oil
175g/6oz/¾ cup brown butter (see page 58)

Allow the meat to come to room temperature; this takes about 2 hours if the meat has been in the refrigerator.

Set up a fire pit with a grill grate, using firewood, and let the fire burn down to a bed of embers. Preheat the oven or a grill with a lid to 150°C/300°F/gas 2.

Rub the beef all over with sea salt. Sear on all sides over high heat; if any fat drops onto the embers it will create flames, so have some tongs ready to move the meat out of the flames when necessary.

Place the beef in a roasting pan and cook in the oven for about 1–1½ hours until the internal temperature reaches 54°C/130°F; if you don't have a cooking thermometer, test by pressing the meat firmly with your finger: it should feel quite soft but should spring back slightly to the touch. Remove from the oven and leave to rest for 30 minutes. Keep the fire burning while the beef is in the oven. Alternatively, if your firepit has a lid, put the lid on and cook for 1–1½ hours.

To make the brown butter emulsion, bring a large pan of water to the boil. Carefully add the eggs and cook for 2 minutes. Drain and cool the eggs in iced water, then peel them.

Put the eggs in a bowl, add the vinegar and salt, and mash to a smooth paste. Pour in the oil a few drops at a time, whisking constantly, until the mixture emulsifies. Repeat with the brown butter.

Using a mandolin, slice the radishes, onion and fennel thinly and place in a bowl of iced water for 15 minutes. Drain the vegetables thoroughly and mix with the salad leaves. Mix the lemon juice and olive oil, season with salt and toss with the salad.

Cut the meat off the bone and sear on the grill grate over high heat to create a dry, freshly grilled surface. Slice the meat into 1cm/½in-thick slices and serve with your choice of flavoured salt, the mixed salad and the brown butter emulsion.

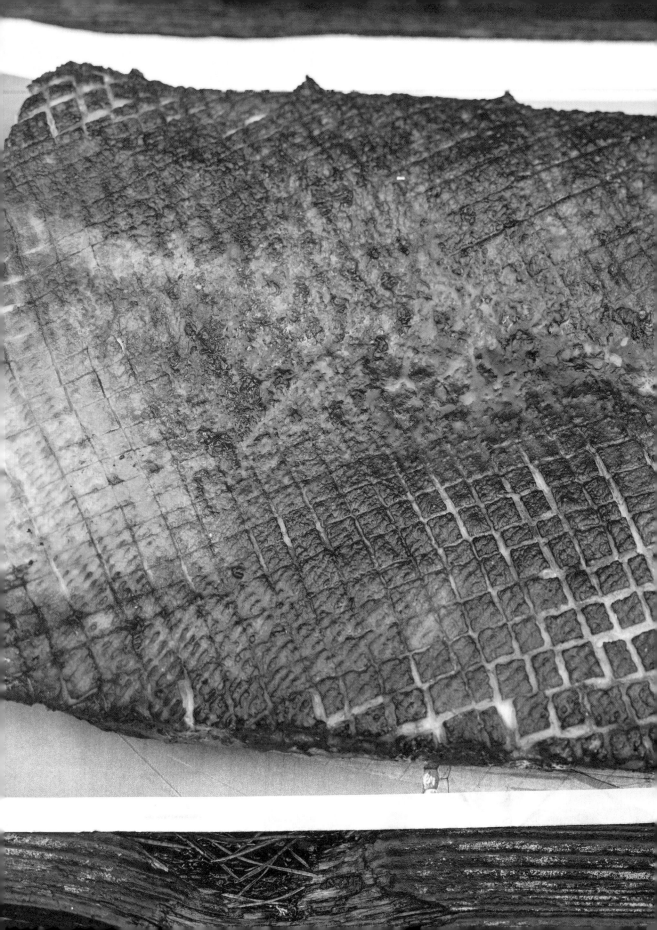

HOT-SMOKED PORK BELLY

Serves 8–10

3.5–4.5kg/8–10lb pork belly
450ml/16fl oz/2 cups water
115g/4oz/6 tbsp salt
85g/3oz/scant ½ cup brown sugar
2 tbsp ground fennel seeds
3 tbsp ground coriander seeds
1 tbsp mustard powder
2 tbsp black peppercorns
4 garlic cloves, peeled and crushed
1 onion, roughly chopped

Bring the water to the boil, add all the remaining ingredients and boil until the salt and sugar have dissolved. Leave until completely cold. Put the pork belly in a large glass or plastic container, cover with the brine and store in the refrigerator for 3 days. Turn it over once a day.

Prepare a smoker – or a grill over firewood – allowing space so the meat does not come into direct contact with the heat. Preheat to 100–120°C/210–250°F. Lift the pork belly out of the brine and rinse under running cold water for 5 minutes, then dry thoroughly with a paper towel. Put the meat in the smoker, fat side up, and smoke for about 3–4 hours until the internal temperature reaches 72°C/163°F.

Remove from the smoker and let sit for 20 minutes. To serve as it is, score the fat and place the meat fat side down in a cast-iron pan. Cook over low heat for about 10 minutes until golden brown, then turn and cook the other side for 5–8 minutes.

PORK BELLY, MISO AND CARAMELIZED ONION

One of my favourite ingredients from the Japanese kitchen is miso, fermented soybean paste. In this recipe I combine it with the traditional Swedish flavours of pork and sweet caramelized onion.

Serves 4

280g/10oz/1¾ cups chopped onion
55g/2oz/4 tbsp butter
4 potatoes, peeled, boiled until almost tender and cut into roughly 1.5cm/½in cubes
2 tsp fresh thyme leaves
3 tbsp miso paste
1 tsp freshly ground black pepper
1 fennel bulb
4 pieces of hot-smoked pork belly (see left), about 150g/5oz each
5 tsp finely chopped fresh parsley

Put the onion and butter in a saucepan. Cover with a lid and cook over low heat until the onion is translucent. Remove the lid and continue cooking over low heat until it is caramelized, about 45 minutes. Add the potatoes, thyme, miso and pepper, and cook gently for a further 5 minutes.

Using a mandolin, slice the fennel thinly and place in a bowl of iced water.

Heat a cast-iron pan over high heat. Score the fat on the pork belly and place fat-side down in the cast-iron pan. Cook over low heat until golden brown, about 8–10 minutes. Turn and cook on the other side for 5–8 minutes.

Drain the fennel. Serve the caramelized onion and fennel with a piece of pork, sprinkled with parsley.

EMBER-BAKED JACKET POTATO WITH CARAMELIZED ONION AND PORK

This is a good way to use up any leftover pork belly (see page 148), or you can use bacon instead. You can precook the potatoes at home and take them with you on a picnic to heat up in the picnic fire.

Serves 4

4 large potatoes
280g/10oz/1¾ cups onion, chopped
55g/2oz/4 tbsp butter
2 tsp fresh thyme leaves
3 tbsp miso paste
1 tsp freshly ground black pepper
150g/5oz hot-smoked pork belly (see page 148)
    or smoked bacon, cut into 5mm/¼in dice
1 fennel bulb
5 tsp finely chopped fresh parsley

Start the fire with firewood.

Wrap the potatoes in foil, place in the embers and cook for about 1–1½ hours. Keep feeding the fire to ensure there is enough heat around the potatoes.

Put the onion and butter in a saucepan. Cover with a lid and cook over low heat until the onion is translucent. Remove the lid and continue cooking over low heat until it is caramelized, about 45 minutes. Add the thyme, miso and black pepper and cook gently for a further 5 minutes.

Put the diced pork or bacon in a cold pan and place over medium heat. Cook until golden brown, then add to the onion mixture.

Using a mandolin, slice the fennel thinly and place in a bowl of iced water.

Drain the fennel. Unwrap the ember-baked potatoes and serve with the caramelized onion mixture, raw fennel and parsley.

BEEF RYDBERG

A luxurious variation of *pytt-i-panna*, a classic Swedish dish made from leftover meat, pan fried with onions and potatoes. This dish, made from tender beef and served with a mustard cream sauce, is believed to have originated at the (now closed) Hotel Rydberg in Stockholm in the 19th century. Another version, with a little cream added at the end, is called Biff Greta. This is typically served as a late-night dinner, for example at weddings, accompanied by pickled cucumber and raw egg yolks.

Serves 4

4 tbsp homemade sour cream (see page 104)
2 tsp Dijon mustard
1 tbsp wholegrain mustard
900g/2lb waxy potatoes
900g/2lb beef fillet (tenderloin) or sirloin
2 onions, chopped
200g/7oz/¾ cup butter
5 tbsp vegetable oil
salt and freshly ground black pepper
1 bunch of parsley, chopped
4 egg yolks

Combine the sour cream and both mustards in a bowl. Cover and chill until ready to serve.

Cut the potatoes into 2.5cm/1in cubes and rinse in cold water to wash away the starch, changing the water two or three times. Drain and leave to dry on paper towels.

Cut the beef into 2.5cm/1in cubes and allow to come to room temperature.

Put the onions and 85g/3oz/6 tablespoons of the butter in a saucepan over medium heat and cook for about 30 minutes until caramelized.

Heat a large cast-iron pan over medium heat with 4 tablespoons of the oil. Add the potato cubes and pan-fry to lightly colour on all sides. Add 55g/2oz/4 tablespoons of the butter and continue cooking until the potatoes are golden brown and soft in the middle. Remove from the pan and season with salt.

Reheat the cast-iron pan over high heat. Add 2 teaspoons of oil and add the meat. Sear on one side for about 2 minutes. Add the remaining butter and cook the meat on all sides to medium–rare. Remove from the pan and leave to rest for 3 minutes.

Put the meat and potatoes back in the pan, add the onions and heat through. Season with salt and pepper. Sprinkle with parsley and serve with raw egg yolks and the mustard cream.

VENISON MEATBALLS WITH RED CABBAGE SALAD AND BLACKENED APPLE

In Sweden, we make these meatballs with elk, our most famous game meat. Reindeer meat or venison will work equally well. You will need to prepare the raw red cabbage salad a day in advance. We usually serve these with lingonberries; alternatively, serve with preserved redcurrants (see page 48).

Serves 4

115g/4oz/½ cup butter
1 onion, finely chopped
5 tsp fresh breadcrumbs
90ml/3fl oz/6 tbsp milk
90ml/3fl oz/6 tbsp double (heavy) cream
2 tsp salt
½ tsp ground black pepper
½ tsp finely ground juniper berries
700g/1½lb coarsely minced (ground) venison, elk or
    reindeer meat
280g/10oz minced (ground) pork
350g/12oz/3½ cups frozen lingonberries mixed with
    115g/4oz/generous ½ cup caster (superfine) sugar
    (see page 100), to serve

Raw red cabbage salad
450g/1lb red cabbage
40g/1½oz/2 tbsp salt
90ml/3fl oz/6 tbsp red wine vinegar
150g/5oz/¾ cup sugar
1 star anise
2 cloves
1 small cinnamon stick
1 bay leaf

Caramelized red cabbage salad
450g/1lb red cabbage
30g/1oz/2 tbsp butter
1 red onion, sliced
55g/2oz/¼ cup soft brown sugar

4 tbsp red wine vinegar
1 bay leaf
salt

Blackened apples
2 apples
30g/1oz/2 tbsp butter

Mashed potato
90ml/3fl oz/6 tbsp milk
90ml/3fl oz/6 tbsp double (heavy) cream
1 bay leaf
3 black peppercorns
½ tsp ground nutmeg
skin of ½ onion
450g/1lb potatoes, peeled
55g/2oz/4 tbsp butter

To make the raw red cabbage salad, slice the cabbage thinly – easiest on a mandolin – and rinse in cold water. Drain and place in a bowl with the salt. Mix well, cover with clingfilm and store in the refrigerator for 3–4 hours. In a saucepan, combine the vinegar, sugar and spices in 140ml/5fl oz/generous ½ cup of water and bring to the boil over medium heat, stirring until the sugar has dissolved. Remove from the heat, leave for 10 minutes and then strain to remove the whole spices. Leave to cool. Rinse the cabbage in cold running water for 5 minutes. Drain well. Place in a bowl, add the sugar and vinegar liquid, and store in the refrigerator for 24 hours.

To make the meatballs, heat half the butter in a saucepan over medium–high heat, add the onion and sauté until soft but not coloured. Remove from the heat and leave to cool.

Put the breadcrumbs in a bowl, add the milk and cream and leave to soak for 5 minutes.

Combine the onion, salt, pepper and juniper, then add both meats and mix well (but don't overwork, otherwise it will get too warm and split). Cover and store in the refrigerator for 30 minutes.

To make the caramelized red cabbage salad, cut out the core of the cabbage and cut the cabbage into roughly 2cm/¾in cubes. Melt the butter in a saucepan over medium–high heat. Add the cabbage and onion and sauté until soft. Add the sugar, vinegar and bay leaf and simmer until all the liquid has evaporated and the mixture starts to caramelize. Season with salt to taste.

To make the blackened apples, cut each apple into 16 wedges. Spread the apple in a cast-iron pan and place over medium–high heat. Roast until the apples begin to release liquid. Turn up the heat and caramelize the surface until almost burned. Remove from the heat, add the butter, let it melt and mix it around with the apples.

To make the mashed potato, heat the milk, cream, bay leaf, peppercorns, nutmeg and onion skin in a saucepan over medium heat to just below boiling point. Remove from the heat, cover and leave for 20 minutes. Meanwhile, cook the potatoes in salted boiling water until tender. Drain and leave in the pan with the lid off until the steam disappears. Strain the creamy liquid. Mash the potatoes, add the liquid and whisk to combine; whisk as little as possible to prevent the potatoes becoming gluey. Add the butter and season with salt to taste.

Preheat the oven to 150°C/300°F/gas 2. Wet your hands and shape the meat mixture into small meatballs. Heat the remaining butter in a frying pan over medium heat and fry the meatballs until golden brown all over. Transfer the meatballs to a baking tray and cook through in the oven for about 10 minutes.

Serve the meatballs with caramelized red cabbage and raw red cabbage salad, blackened apples, mashed potato and lingonberries.

SMOKED DUCK BREAST WITH
SPICY CURED CABBAGE

For this dish, the cured cabbage needs to be started 2 days in advance.

Serves 4

2 duck breasts, each weighing about 450g/1lb
85g/3oz/scant ½ cup caster (superfine) sugar
55g/2oz/3 tbsp salt
300ml/10fl oz/1¼ cups water
12 allspice berries
2 cinnamon sticks
10 cloves
3cm/1¼in piece of fresh ginger, peeled and chopped
55g/2oz/scant ½ cup cashew nuts, roasted
12 pieces of cured cabbage (see below)
120ml/4fl oz/½ cup dipping sauce (see below)
1 bunch of coriander, leaves only

Cured cabbage
1–2 large pointed cabbages
30g/1oz/1½ tbsp salt
2 red chillies, deseeded
4 garlic cloves, peeled
½ onion, roughly chopped
2 tsp grated fresh ginger
1 tbsp caster (superfine) sugar
2 tbsp fish sauce

Dipping sauce
40g/1½oz/3 tbsp palm sugar
150ml/5fl oz/scant ⅔ cup water
150ml/5fl oz/scant ⅔ cup fish sauce
1 tsp freshly squeezed lime juice
1 tbsp rice wine vinegar
4 tbsp Japanese soy sauce
1 tbsp finely chopped deseeded red chilli

Begin by preparing the cured cabbage. Set up a firepit with a grill grate, using firewood. Cut the cabbage into large wedges – three pieces per person. Place on the grill grate, sliced surface down, and sear over medium heat. Alternatively, sear in a hot pan. Remove from the grill, rub salt into the cabbage and store in the refrigerator for 24 hours.

The next day, combine the chillies, garlic, onion, ginger, sugar and fish sauce in a blender and blend to a smooth paste. Rinse the cabbage in cold water, and dry with paper towels. Pour over the spicy paste and store in the refrigerator for 12–24 hours.

For the duck, put the sugar, salt, water, allspice, cinnamon, cloves and ginger in a saucepan. Bring to the boil over medium heat and simmer for 5 minutes. Remove from the heat and leave for 30 minutes. Strain and leave until completely cool.

Put the duck breasts in a bowl, cover with the marinade and store in the refrigerator for 4 hours.

To make the dipping sauce, put the palm sugar and water in a saucepan over medium–high heat and bring to the boil until the sugar has dissolved. Leave to cool. Add the remaining ingredients and store in a jar in a cool, dark place.

Preheat the smoker to 100°C/210°F. Pour off the marinade and dry the duck with paper towels. Score the duck skin with a sharp knife. Smoke for about 30 minutes until the internal temperature reaches 58°C/135°F. If you don't have a cooking thermometer, test by pressing the duck breast firmly with your finger: the meat should feel quite soft but should spring back slightly to the touch. Rest for 5–10 minutes.

Heat the cabbage in the smoker for 10 minutes. Slice the duck breast and serve with wedges of cabbage, the dipping sauce, roasted cashew nuts, and coriander leaves. You could also serve basmati rice as an accompaniment.

WHOLE GRILLED TURBOT WITH CREAMY POTATO SALAD, SMOKED BUTTER AND CURRY PICKLES

This is kind of messy to serve, but is fun and delicious. To cook the fish, you will need a wide fire pit grill with a lid. Set up a buffet table close to the grill and let your friends or family serve themselves.

Serves 4

1 whole turbot, weighing about 1.8kg/4lb, cleaned
55g/2oz/3 tbsp salt
2 lemons, cut in half
creamy potato salad (see below)
450g/1lb curry pickles (see page 52)
85g/3oz/6 tbsp smoked butter (see page 58)
1 bunch of dill

Creamy potato salad
450g/1lb cold cooked potatoes
85g/3oz/6 tbsp mayonnaise (see page 90)
2 tbsp crème fraîche
2 tsp red wine vinegar

Rub the salt all over the fish and leave at room temperature for 1 hour.

To make the creamy potato salad: cut the potatoes into roughly 1cm/½in cubes. Place in a serving bowl and fold in the mayonnaise, crème fraîche and vinegar. Season with salt to taste. Chill until ready to serve.

In a wide grill (with a grill grate and lid), light the fire in a corner of the grill. It is important that the fish does not come into contact with direct heat. Dry the fish with a paper towel. Place on the grill grate, away from the side with the fire, and cover with the lid. Cook for about 1 hour (checking on a thermometer, keep the heat in the covered grill at around 120–130°C/250–265°F); make sure you keep the fire going. The fish is done when the internal temperature of the thickest part reaches 54°C/130°F. If you do not have a cooking thermometer, make a cut in the thickest part of the fish: it should be white and cooked all the way through. Towards the end of cooking, place the lemon halves over the fire, to grill for a minute or so.

Remove the skin and serve directly from the grill grate with the grilled lemon halves, potato salad, curry pickled vegetables, smoked butter and a sprinkling of dill.

HAY-FLAMED COD WITH BROWN BUTTER, PINK PEPPER-PICKLED CUCUMBER AND MISO-ROASTED POTATOES

Hay flaming is a fun way of cooking and gives a nice taste of an open fire to the food. Make sure the hay is really dry.

Serves 4

4 pieces of cod, about 175g/6oz each, skin on
2 tsp salt
115g/4oz/½ cup butter, softened
4 tsp miso paste
900g/2lb new potatoes, cleaned
½ cucumber
5 tsp icing (confectioners') sugar
3 tbsp *ättika* (Swedish white vinegar),
    or white wine vinegar
2 tsp pink peppercorns, roasted and crushed
4 tsp chopped fresh dill
1 bunch of fresh, clean, dry hay
    (approx. 2 big handfuls)
115g/4oz/½ cup brown butter (see page 58)

Rub the salt over the fish and leave at room temperature for 30 minutes.

Preheat the oven to 180°C/350°F/gas 4.

Combine 85g/3oz/6 tablespoons of the butter with the miso paste. Put the potatoes in a roasting pan and dot with the miso butter. Roast in the oven for about 30 minutes, stirring every 10 minutes, until cooked through. Set aside.

Using a mandolin, slice the cucumber finely and mix with the icing sugar, vinegar, pink pepper and chopped dill. Set aside.

Turn the oven down to 120°C/250°F/gas ½.

Dry the fish with paper towels, then spread with the remaining 30g/1oz/2 tablespoons of butter. Place it on a fire-resistant tray, skin side up. Cook in the oven for about 30 minutes or until the internal temperature reaches 54°C/130°F. If you do not have a cooking thermometer, make a cut in the thickest part of the fish: it should be white and cooked all the way through.

Remove from the oven and take the tray somewhere where it is safe to set it alight. Cover the fish with hay and set the hay on fire, using a piece of burning firewood or a blowtorch. Make sure all the hay is burned. Brush off the ash and remove the fish skin. Serve with the miso-roasted potatoes, cucumber and brown butter.

SOTAD STRÖMMING
BLACKENED HERRING, PICKLED GOOSEBERRIES AND SOURDOUGH CROUTONS

In Sweden, I use Baltic herrings, which are about 15cm/6in long; if you buy larger herrings, about 25cm/10in long, you will need only one per person. Fresh mackerel could be used in place of herring. Instead of cooking the fish over an open fire as here, you could use a really hot cast-iron pan.

Serves 4

12 fresh herrings, gutted
salt
200g/7oz unsalted butter
4 slices of sourdough bread (see page 64),
    cut into 1cm/½in cubes
85g/3oz pickled gooseberries (see page 46)

Start the fire with birch firewood and burn down until you get a solid glow over the entire surface of the firewood.

Clean the herrings inside and out, dry with paper towels and season with salt.

Heat the butter in a large cast-iron pan over medium heat and cook the cubes of bread until crisp and golden brown. Using a slotted spoon, lift out the bread and drain on paper towels. Keep the browned butter in the pan and season with salt.

Turn a glowing surface of the firewood face-up and place the herrings on top. Cook for 3–4 minutes on both sides. You may need to do this in batches.

Serve the herrings topped with the browned butter, croutons and pickled gooseberries. If you like, you can also serve with boiled potatoes tossed with dill, and crusty bread or *Knäckebröd* (see page 68).

STONE-ROASTED LAMB, HASSELBACK POTATOES, KALE AND TARRAGON EMULSION

The potatoes are named after the restaurant Hasselbacken in Stockholm, Sweden, where they were introduced in the 1940s. The restaurant opened in 1748 and is now part of a hotel of the same name.

Serves 4

1.3kg/3lb potatoes, preferably oval shaped
salt
115g/4oz/½ cup butter, at room temperature
6 tsp dried breadcrumbs
2 lamb racks, each weighing about 450g/1lb
1 bunch of kale, washed and drained
2 shallots, chopped

Tarragon emulsion
175ml/6fl oz/¾ cup vegetable oil
4 tsp chopped fresh tarragon
2 egg yolks
1 tsp Dijon mustard
1 tsp salt
175g/6oz/¾ cup brown butter (see page 58), melted and cooled slightly
1 tbsp sherry vinegar

To make the tarragon emulsion, put the oil and tarragon in a blender and blend thoroughly. Put the egg yolks in a wide bowl and add the mustard and salt. Using a balloon whisk, beat until pale and creamy. Keep whisking and pour in the tarragon oil a few drops at a time until the mixture emulsifies. Whisk in the brown butter in the same way; if it gets too thick, add a few drops of cold water. Finally, whisk in the vinegar. Chill until ready to serve.

Set up a fire pit surrounded by large stones. Start the fire with firewood, close enough to the stones to heat them up.

Preheat the oven to 200°C/400°F/gas 6.

Peel the potatoes and cut downwards into very thin slices, stopping just before cutting all the way through, so the slices remain connected along the bottom of the potato. This requires careful knife work but is not difficult. Season the potatoes with salt. Spread 85g/3oz of the butter over the sliced surfaces of the potatoes and sprinkle the breadcrumbs on top. Place in a roasting pan and bake in the oven for about 40 minutes until golden brown and soft in the middle. Remove from the oven.

Remove from the fire a stone large enough to hold the lamb racks. Season the lamb with salt and sear on both sides on the hot stone. Place the lamb on the side of the fire (where the temperature should be about 90–120°C/190–250°F) and cook for about 20–40 minutes, until the internal temperature reaches 58°C/135°F; the lamb should be medium-rare. Rest it for 5–10 minutes.

Remove the stems from the kale and cut it into pieces about 5cm/2in square. Heat a cast-iron pan over medium heat. Add the remaining butter and the kale and sauté for 5 minutes. Add the shallots and sauté for 2 minutes.

Carve the lamb into cutlets and serve with the hasselback potatoes, kale and tarragon emulsion.

EMBER-DUSTED LAMB, BRUSSELS SPROUTS, SQUASH, CRANBERRIES AND GRILLED APPLE COMPOTE

The technique of rolling the meat in the embers after cooking lends a delicious taste of the fire to this simple lamb dish.

Serves 4

150g/5oz/1½ cups dried cranberries
6 shallots, peeled
350g/12oz butternut squash, peeled and deseeded
350g/12oz Brussels sprouts, trimmed and cut in half
3 tbsp vegetable oil
salt
450g/1lb small potatoes, cleaned
450g/1lb lamb rump, or boneless leg
3 sprigs fresh thyme

Grilled apple compote
3 dessert apples
4 tsp sugar
1 tbsp butter
1 cinnamon stick

Soak the dried cranberries in water.

Preheat the oven to 200°C/400°F/gas 6.

Cut the shallots in half lengthways. Heat a cast-iron pan over high heat. Add the shallots, cut side down, and sear until almost burned. Remove from the heat and set aside.

Cut the butternut squash into cubes. Put the squash, Brussels sprouts and 1 tablespoon of oil in a roasting pan, season with salt and turn to coat in the oil. Roast in the oven for about 30 minutes. Remove and set aside.

Season the potatoes with salt, roast in the oven with 1 tablespoon of oil for about 30 minutes.

Turn the oven down to 120°C/250°F/gas ½. Set up a fire pit, using firewood.

Heat a cast-iron pan over medium heat. Season the lamb with salt and sear on all sides in the cast-iron pan with 1 tablespoon of oil. Put the pan in the oven and bake until the internal temperature reaches 58°C/135°F, about 45 minutes. If you do not have a cooking thermometer, test by pressing the meat firmly with your finger: it should feel quite soft but should spring back slightly to the touch. Remove from the oven, wrap in foil and leave to rest for 15 minutes at room temperature.

To make the apple compote, cut each apple into eight wedges and cut out the cores. Grill the apples over medium heat until golden brown. Melt the sugar in a saucepan over a medium–high heat until golden brown – do not stir the sugar until it is golden brown. Add the apples, butter and cinnamon, cover with a lid and bring to the boil. Remove the lid and simmer for 5–8 minutes; try to keep a little crispness in the centre of the apples.

Drain the cranberries and combine with the potatoes and roasted vegetables. Heat in the oven for 5 minutes.

Unwrap the lamb and dry with paper towels. Roll the lamb in the embers for about 45 seconds. Shake and remove the larger pieces of ash from the meat. Cut the lamb into 2cm/¾in slices and serve with the cranberries, vegetables and apple compote.

OPEN FIRE-ROASTED POUSSINS, EMBER-BAKED CARROTS AND CHIMICHURRI

Use small young chickens (poussins) and spatchcock them by opening them out flat, which reduces the cooking time. If you prefer, you can cook the poussins in the oven and finish roasting them over the fire.

Serves 4

2 lemons
55g/2oz salt
½ tsp ground cardamom
4 poussins, each weighing about 700g/1½lb
900g/2lb carrots
6 tsp chopped fresh parsley
1 tsp chopped deseeded red chilli
1 tsp chopped fresh thyme
1 tsp chopped garlic
120ml/4fl oz extra virgin olive oil

Start the fire with firewood. It should be at least 60cm/2ft wide (big enough for 4 poussins).

Grate the zest of 1 lemon and mix it with the salt and cardamom.

Using poultry shears, cut out the backbones from the poussins. Turn each chicken breast-side up and open it out flat. Rub the chickens with the salt mixture and leave for 1 hour at room temperature.

Stick two parallel skewers into each chicken, starting through the legs (the legs need more heat to cook and are therefore placed closer to the fire than the breasts). Place the chickens on the side of the fire, turning them over every 20 minutes. The total cooking time will be about 1–2 hours, depending on the temperature of the fire. Cook until the internal temperature reaches 72°C/163°F. If you do not have a cooking thermometer, pierce the thickest part of the leg with a skewer: the juices should run clear and golden, with no trace of pink.

After setting up the chicken, place the carrots in the embers and cook until soft, which will take about 45–60 minutes.

To make the chimichurri, mix the parsley, chilli, thyme, garlic and olive oil in a bowl. Set aside. Cut the lemons in half.

When the carrots are soft, remove them from the embers. Peel off the burnt skin and cut in half. Season with salt. Serve the chicken with ember-baked carrots, chimichurri and lemon halves.

Spatchcock the chickens as above, rub them with the salt, lemon and cardamom mixture and leave for 1 hour at room temperature.

Preheat the oven to 150°C/300°F/gas 2.

Put the chickens in a large roasting pan and cook in the oven for about 1–1½ hours until the internal temperature reaches 72°C/163°F.

Stick two parallel skewers into each chicken, starting through the legs. Place the chickens on the side of the fire and roast until golden brown.

RHUBARB-GLAZED PORK RIBS

Great finger food means greasy fingers. You'll need a lot of paper towels, and some small bowls of water with a couple of slices of lemon to rinse your fingers. You will also need about 3–4 handfuls of wood smoking chips. This is great served with an apple and watercress salad (see page 135).

Serves 4

1.3–1.8kg/3–4lb meaty pork spare ribs
30g/1oz/1½ tbsp hay salt (see page 36)
caramelized walnut, apple and watercress salad
  (see page 135)

Rhubarb glaze
900g/2lb rhubarb, roughly sliced into
  2cm/¾in pieces
200ml/7fl oz/generous ¾ cup apple juice
5 tsp cornflour (cornstarch)
2 tbsp water
115g/4oz/6 tbsp honey
6 tsp Dijon mustard
1 tbsp white wine vinegar

Rub the hay salt into the ribs and set aside at room temperature for 30 minutes. Preheat the grill or oven to 140°C/275°F/gas 1.

Place the ribs on a baking tray and cook in the oven, turning them every 30 minutes or so, for about 3 hours or until tender. To test, stick a small knife into the thickest part of the meat; when the meat offers no resistance and the knife pulls out easily, the meat is ready. Remove from the oven and wrap in foil.

While the meat is cooking, make the rhubarb glaze. Put the rhubarb in a saucepan with the apple juice. Bring to the boil and simmer for 15 minutes or until the rhubarb is very tender. Strain through a sieve into a jug, pressing the pulp with the back of a spoon to extract as much liquid as possible. Discard the pulp.

In a saucepan, mix the cornflour and water until the cornflour has dissolved. Add the rhubarb liquid and cook over medium heat, stirring until thickened and bubbly; continue to cook and stir for 2 minutes. Remove from the heat and stir in the honey, mustard and vinegar. Leave to cool.

Preheat a smoker to 145°C/295°F. Alternatively, if using a fire pit, soak the smoking chips in water for 30 minutes. Prepare the fire pit with a grill grate, using firewood – allowing space to place the ribs without direct contact with the heat. Let the fire burn down to embers. Pile the embers on one side and sprinkle the soaked smoking chips on top of the embers. Place the ribs on the grill grate over the embers, avoiding direct contact with the heat.

Reheat the rhubarb glaze over medium heat, stirring constantly, until almost boiling. Brush the ribs with some of the glaze and place in the smoker, meat side up. Smoke for about 45 minutes, brushing with glaze every 10 minutes.

Remove from the smoker, cut into portions and brush with more rhubarb glaze. Serve with walnut, apple and watercress salad.

FLAMED HALIBUT AND CITRUS
WITH MUSHROOM AND SALSIFY NOODLES

The *flambadou* has been used in France since medieval times. It is a cone-shaped iron tool with a very long handle that is heated in the fire until red-hot; just before service some fat or marrow is added; the super-hot fat is then poured over a piece of meat or a whole chicken that has been roasting on a spit (see also pages 32 and 237). In this recipe, we use it to cook sliced fresh halibut.

The mushroom and salsify noodles can also be served on their own as a filling supper. Illustrated separately overleaf.

Serves 4

Mushroom and salsify noodles
450ml/16fl oz/2 cups double (heavy) cream
skin of 1 onion
¼ tsp ground nutmeg
1 bay leaf
1.3kg/3lb salsify
4 tsp lemon juice
salt
30g/1oz/2 tbsp butter
1 shallot, finely chopped
450g/1lb chanterelles (or other seasonal
    mushrooms), cleaned
1 tbsp chopped fresh parsley

Flamed halibut
450g/1lb halibut loin
55g/2oz/4 tbsp beef tallow cleaned, cut
    into 2cm/¾in cubes, at room temperature
    (alternatively, beef dripping could be substituted)
1 lime, halved
1 lemon, peeled, cut into segments (ensure no white
    pith remains), then halved again
½ tsp finely chopped dried citrus peel (see page 54)
1 bunch of chervil sprigs

Set up a fire pit with firewood. Fill the *flambadou* with glowing embers and place in the fire.

In a saucepan, combine the cream, onion skin, nutmeg and bay leaf and bring to the boil over medium heat. Simmer until reduced to about 200ml/7fl oz/about ¾ cup. Remove from the heat, strain the cream and set aside.

Peel the salsify and place in a bowl of water with the lemon juice. Using a vegetable peeler, cut the salsify into noodle-like strips. Bring a large pan of water to the boil and add salt. Blanch the salsify in the boiling water for 3 minutes. Drain and cool in iced water, then drain and dry on paper towels.

Heat a cast-iron pan over high heat. Add the butter, shallot and chanterelles, and sauté for 3 minutes. Remove from the heat and add the reduced cream and salsify noodles.

Slice the halibut 'sashimi style' and place on a fire-resistant platter.

Take the *flambadou* out of the fire and pour out the embers. It should be red hot. Carefully place some of the tallow (or beef dripping) in the *flambadou* and quickly turn it over the flames so it catches fire. Hold the *flambadou* over the halibut and drip the hot fat over the fish. (For alternative method without a *flambadou*, see page 124.)

Squeeze the lime juice over the halibut. Sprinkle the dried citrus peel, lemon segments and chervil on top. Serve with the creamy mushroom and salsify noodles on the side, sprinkled with the chopped parsley (pictured overleaf).

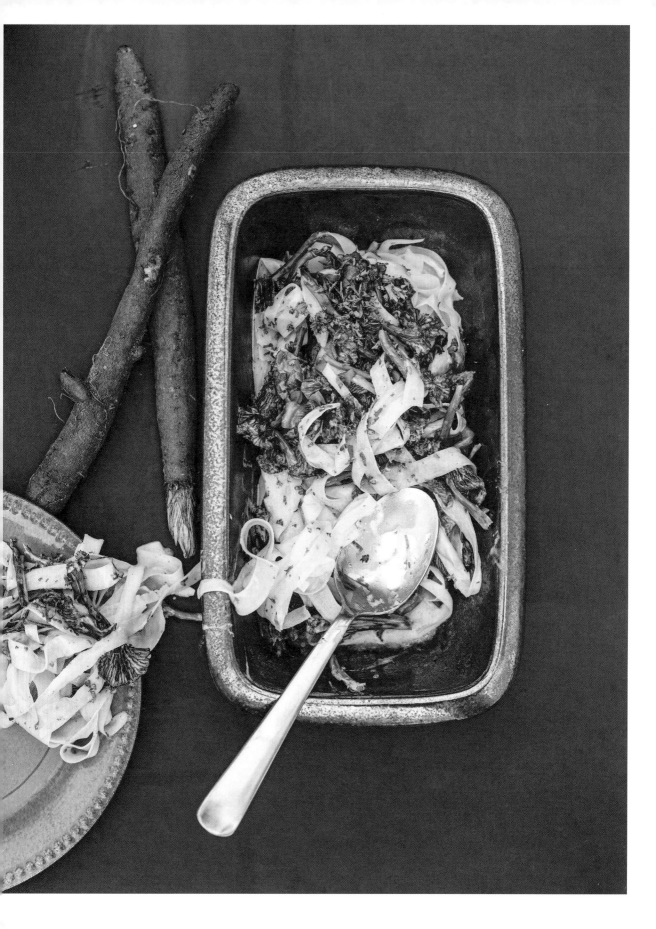

CAST-IRON PAN-FRIED LOBSTER, SAFFRON MAYONNAISE AND PICKLED VEGETABLES

When shelling the lobster, try to keep the brownish meat you find in the head cavity – this is actually the liver of the lobster; it doesn't look great, but it adds great flavour to the dish, when cooked in butter.

Serves 4

225g/8oz/¾ cup salt
4 lobsters
55g/2oz/4 tbsp butter
450g/1lb pickled vegetables (see page 52)
2 lemons, cut in half
8 slices of sourdough bread (see page 64), toasted

Saffron mayonnaise
pinch of saffron strands
1 tbsp Cognac
2 egg yolks
1 tsp Dijon mustard
1 tsp salt
350ml/12fl oz/1½ cups vegetable oil
4 tsp freshly squeezed lemon juice

First, make the saffron mayonnaise, soak the saffron in the Cognac for about 30 minutes.

Put the egg yolks in a wide bowl, add the mustard and salt, and beat, using a balloon whisk, until pale and creamy. Keep whisking and pour in the oil a few drops at a time until the mixture emulsifies. Add the lemon juice. Chill until ready to serve.

Bring a large pan of water (large enough to fit all the lobsters, or to cook 1 lobster at a time) to the boil and add the salt.

Put a large cutting board on a folded tea towel to keep it stable. Using a large knife, place the knife tip to the centre of the lobster shell, about 2cm/¾in above the eyes, and cut firmly down to kill the lobster instantly. Add the lobsters to the boiling water and cook for 3 minutes. Remove and place in iced water for 5–8 minutes.

Remove the lobster meat from the shells, keeping the tail and claw meat separate. Scrape out the 'lobster butter' (the smooth brownish or greenish meat that is actually the lobster's liver, also known as the tomalley) from the heads and set aside. Cut the tails in half lengthways and remove the black vein.

Heat a cast-iron pan over medium heat. Add the butter and lobster claw meat and pan-fry for 2 minutes. Add the tails, cut sides down, and cook for 2 minutes. Add the 'lobster butter' and gently combine with the butter. Cook for 1 minute.

Serve the lobster with saffron mayonnaise, pickled vegetables, lemon halves and toasted sourdough bread.

KRÄFTSKIVA
CRAYFISH PARTY

In August, the Swedes traditionally celebrate
with a crayfish party. We dine in the garden,
eating freshly cooked crayfish, drinking
snaps (aquavit) and beer, and wearing
ridiculous paper hats. In order to keep the
crayfish population sustainable, the season
is restricted, opening in mid to late August.
The crayfish are caught during the night, in
cages baited with fish. They are cooked alive
in boiling salted water with dill flowers and
lager beer and eaten with the fingers, slurping
the flesh from the shells. I usually serve
freshly cooked langoustines, too, and even a
crab or two if I can get them. The traditional
accompaniments are spicy cheese, butter and
crispy bread.

Serves 4–6

900g/2lb cooked freshwater crayfish
900g/2lb cooked langoustines
175g/6oz/¾ cup *potkäs* (see page 62)
115g/4oz/½ cup butter
8 pieces of crispy bread, such as *tunbröd*
   (see page 70)

DESSERTS

PANCAKE CAKE WITH RHUBARB AND VANILLA

The number one favourite at Swedish kids' birthday parties. Adding a little rum to the crème pâtissière makes it lighter and more refreshing for grown-ups.

Serves 8

Crème pâtissière
1 vanilla pod
325ml/11fl oz/generous 1⅓ cups milk
150ml/5fl oz/⅔ cup double (heavy) cream
85g/3oz/scant ½ cup caster (superfine) sugar
1 egg
3 egg yolks
40g/1½oz/5 tbsp cornflour (cornstarch)
2 tbsp dark rum

Pancakes
115g/4oz/scant 1 cup plain (all-purpose) flour
600ml/20fl oz/2½ cups milk
3 eggs
1 tsp salt
115g/4oz/½ cup butter, melted

To assemble
225ml/8fl oz/scant 1 cup double (heavy) cream, whipped
115g/4oz/⅔ cup strawberries or raspberries
115g/4oz preserved rhubarb (see page 48)

First, make the crème pâtissière: split the vanilla pod in half and scrape out the seeds. Put the milk, cream, half of the sugar, the vanilla pod and seeds in a saucepan and heat over medium heat to the point of boiling. Set aside.

Using a balloon whisk, beat the egg, egg yolks and the remaining sugar in a large bowl until pale and creamy. Sift over the cornflour and mix well. Pour about one-third of the hot milk onto the egg mixture and mix well. Pour the mixture into the saucepan with the creamy milk and simmer gently over low heat for 3–4 minutes, stirring constantly until smooth and thick. Remove from the heat and pour into a chilled bowl. Cover with clingfilm and leave to cool. Remove the vanilla pod and stir in the rum.

To make the pancakes, sift the flour into a bowl, add half of the milk and whisk to a smooth batter without lumps of flour. Add the remaining milk, eggs, salt and 30g/1oz of the melted butter and whisk until smooth. Set aside at room temperature for 10 minutes.

Make 16 thin pancakes by pan-frying in melted butter. Leave to cool.

To assemble the cake: fold the whipped cream into the crème pâtissière. Place a pancake on a serving plate, cover with a thin layer of the vanilla cream and repeat until you have used all of the pancakes. Chill in the refrigerator for 1 hour.

Serve with fresh berries, preserved rhubarb and more whipped cream if desired.

BLUEBERRY CRUMBLE

I love picking blueberries, and what could be a better way to serve them than homemade pie?

Serves 8

30g/1oz/2 tbsp butter, at room temperature, for brushing the dish

Filling
900g/2lb/6 cups blueberries
85g/3oz/scant ½ cup caster (superfine) sugar
2 tbsp flour, sifted

Topping
85g/3oz/6 tbsp butter, chilled, cut into cubes
30g/1oz/2 tbsp caster (superfine) sugar
70g/2½oz/generous ½ cup plain (all-purpose) flour
55g/2oz/⅔ cup oatmeal
55g/2oz/scant ½ cup almonds, roughly chopped
1 tbsp ground cardamom

Preheat the oven to 200°C/400°F/gas 6. Brush a 25cm/10in pie dish with butter.

Combine the blueberries, sugar and flour for the filling and place in the pie dish.

Put all the ingredients for the topping in a food processor and blitz until evenly mixed. It should be really dry, so add more flour if needed. Sprinkle evenly over the filling.

Bake for 20–25 minutes. The filling may boil over, so place a tray below the pie in the oven.

Serve hot, with whipped cream or ice cream.

RISALAMANDE WITH SEA BUCKTHORN SAUCE

In Scandinavia, at Christmas time it's traditional to eat boiled rice served with butter, cinnamon, sugar and milk. The next day, we add some sugar and whipped cream and turn the leftovers into a rice pudding, with almonds and orange zest. This is delicious at any time of year, served with a raspberry sauce – or, instead of raspberries, I like to make a sauce with sea buckthorn berries, which we gather in late summer and autumn. In Sweden, we can also buy dried sea buckthorn, which must be soaked overnight; to make this sauce with dried sea buckthorn, use double the amount of sugar and water.

Serves 4

175g/6oz/generous ¾ cup short-grain rice
175ml/6fl oz/¾ cup water
200ml/7fl oz/generous ¾ cup milk
85g/3oz/scant ½ cup caster (superfine) sugar
½ cinnamon stick
¼ vanilla pod, split in half lengthways
1 tsp salt
200ml/7fl oz/generous ¾ cup double (heavy) cream, whipped
grated zest of 1 orange
55g/2oz/scant ½ cup almonds, toasted

Sea buckthorn sauce
85g/3oz sea buckthorn berries
85g/3oz/scant ½ cup caster (superfine) sugar
150ml/5fl oz/⅔ cup water

Put the rice and water in a saucepan. Bring to the boil over medium heat and simmer until all the water is absorbed. Add the milk, sugar, cinnamon, vanilla and salt, and simmer, stirring constantly, until the rice is completely soft, adding more milk if needed. Leave to cool.

To make the sauce, put the berries, sugar and water in a saucepan. Bring to the boil over medium heat and simmer for 10 minutes. Purée in a food processor, strain through a fine sieve and leave to cool. If the sauce is too thick when it is cold, add a little more water.

Fold the whipped cream into the rice. Sprinkle with grated orange zest and toasted almonds and serve with the sea buckthorn sauce.

SOURDOUGH WAFFLES WITH BERRIES

Originally from Belgium, waffles are very popular in Sweden; so popular, in fact, that Waffle Day (25 March) has become a Swedish tradition.

The fermentation starter needs to be made in the evening, the day before you make the waffles. The waffles also need to prove for 4–5 hours before you cook them.

Serves 4

Waffles
300g/10½oz/2¼ cups plain (all-purpose) flour
1 tsp salt
60g/2¼oz/5 tbsp caster (superfine) sugar
1 vanilla pod
500ml/18fl oz/2 cups milk, at 37°C/100°F
3 eggs
100g/3½oz/scant ½ cup butter, melted, plus
   55g/2oz/4 tbsp for brushing the waffle iron
200g/7oz fermentation starter (see below)

Fermentation starter
100g/3½oz/generous ¾ cup plain (all-purpose) flour
100ml/3½fl oz/scant ½ cup water
pinch of fresh yeast

Mint-marinated raspberries
115g/4oz/⅔ cup raspberries
55g/2oz/¼ cup caster (superfine) sugar
6 mint leaves, roughly chopped
grated zest and juice of 1 lime

First, make the fermentation starter: combine all the ingredients in a bowl and whisk to a smooth batter. Cover with a cloth and leave at room temperature for 8–10 hours. It is ready to use when it starts to bubble and you can smell the sourdough aroma.

To make the waffle batter, combine the flour, salt and sugar in a food processor. Split the vanilla pod in half, scrape out the seeds and add them to the milk. Add the vanilla milk and eggs to the food processor and mix to a smooth batter. Pour the batter into a large bowl, add the melted butter and the fermentation starter, and whisk until smooth. Leave to prove at room temperature for 4–5 hours.

To prepare the raspberries, cut them in half and place in a bowl. Combine the sugar, mint and lemon zest in a mortar and grind to a fine powder. Sprinkle the sugar over the raspberries, add the lime juice and stir gently. Set aside for 10 minutes.

Heat up a waffle iron and brush with melted butter. Add some batter to the waffle iron and cook for 3–4 minutes on each side. Serve with mint-marinated raspberries and whipped cream or ice cream.

DOUGHNUTS WITH EMBER-BAKED
APPLES AND MAPLE SYRUP

This is my one of my favourites when spending time with friends and family at a picnic. Bake the apples in the embers while you cook your lunch – or grill the hotdogs – over the fire. If you don't have a cast-iron doughnut pan, you could cook this batter as a thick pancake in a cast-iron frying pan.

Serves 4

4–8 apples
8 tsp maple syrup

Doughnuts
5 eggs
250g/9oz/1¼ cups caster (superfine) sugar
600g/1lb 5oz/5 cups plain (all-purpose) flour
5 tsp baking powder
1 tsp salt
225ml/8fl oz/scant 1 cup double (heavy) cream
225ml/8fl oz/scant 1 cup milk
225g/8oz/1 cup butter, melted
1 tsp ground cinnamon

Wrap the apples in foil and place them in the embers of your fire (or the oven, preheated to 180°C/350°F/gas 4) for 30–40 minutes. Press a small knife into the centre of one apple to make sure it is cooked and soft.

To make the doughnuts, beat the eggs and 225g/8oz/1 cup of the sugar together until pale and creamy. Sift the flour, baking powder and salt into the egg mixture and stir until smooth. Fold in the cream, milk and half of the melted butter. Mix the remaining sugar with the cinnamon and set aside.

Heat a cast-iron doughnut pan over medium heat and add the remaining butter; it will sizzle and brown. Pipe or spoon the doughnut batter into the pan, filling the moulds half way, and cook over medium–high heat for 3–4 minutes, then turn each doughnut over in its mould and continue cooking until browned all over.

Tip the doughnuts out of the pan and roll in the cinnamon sugar. Serve with maple syrup and the ember-baked apples.

HAZELNUT CAKE, WARM CLOUDBERRIES AND YOGURT

Cloudberries have a special place in Swedish gastronomy, with their tart, apricot-like flavour. They grow in the mountain regions of Sweden, and where I grew up, in Jämtland, it is a family tradition to go out on the highland marshes and pick cloudberries on sunny days in August. They look like amber-coloured raspberries, and in this recipe you could replace them with fresh blackberries or raspberries.

Serves 4

Hazelnut cake
200g/7oz/generous ¾ cup unsalted butter,
    plus extra for greasing
200g/7oz/1 cup caster (superfine) sugar
3 eggs
200g/7oz/2⅔ cups light hazelnut flour –
    alternatively, grind 200g/7oz blanched (peeled)
    hazelnuts to a fine powder in a food processor

Cloudberry compote
175g/6oz cloudberries, drained and cleaned
85g/3oz/scant ½ cup caster (superfine) sugar

To serve
55g/2oz/½ cup hazelnuts, toasted
115g/4oz/½ cup natural yogurt

Preheat the oven to 180°C/350°F/gas 4. Grease a 20cm/8in square tin with butter.

To make the hazelnut cake, in a food processor, beat the butter and sugar together until pale and creamy. Keep whisking, and add the eggs one at a time. Fold in the hazelnut flour.

Spoon the mixture into the tin and bake for about 45 minutes. Remove from the oven and leave to cool.

To make the compote, put the berries and sugar in a saucepan and bring to the boil. Reduce the heat and simmer for 5 minutes. Leave to cool slightly.

Slice the hazelnut cake and serve with warm cloudberries, yogurt and toasted hazelnuts.

APPLE PIZZA

Instead of apples, try your favourite fruit toppings, such as apricots, peaches or nectarines, on this fun dessert. Crème pâtissière is a good base, adding a thin layer of rich sweetness.

Makes 8 pizzas

Pizza dough
40g / 1½oz / 2 cakes fresh yeast
300ml / 10fl oz / 1¼ cups lukewarm water
350g / 12oz / scant 3 cups strong white bread flour,
   plus extra for dusting
1 tsp salt
3 tbsp olive oil
2 tsp sugar

Topping
30g / 1oz / 2 tbsp unsalted butter
2 apples, thinly sliced
55g / 2oz / scant ½ cup almonds, chopped
30g / 1oz / 3 tbsp raisins
200g / 7oz crème pâtissière (see page 188)
2 tsp icing (confectioners') sugar

To make the pizza dough: mix the yeast with the water until dissolved. Set aside for 5–10 minutes. Sift the flour and salt into a food processor or a large bowl. Add the yeast liquid, olive oil and sugar. Mix to form a dough and knead – in the processor or by hand – until the dough is smooth and springy. Place the ball of dough in a large, flour-dusted bowl and flour the top of it. Cover the bowl with a damp tea towel and leave in a warm place for about 1 hour until the dough has doubled in size.

Preheat the oven to 200°C / 400°F / gas 6. Lightly flour a large baking sheet.

Turn out the dough onto a floured work surface, then divide it into eight equal pieces. Roll out each piece with a rolling pin, or stretch by hand, to about 5mm / ¼in thick and place on the floured baking sheet. Working in batches (depending on the size of your baking sheet), cook each pizza for about 3 minutes. It should be baked all the way through, but not coloured. Remove from the oven and leave to cool on a wire rack, covering the pizza with a tea towel.

To make the topping, heat a frying pan over high heat and add the butter, apples, almonds and raisins. Stir-fry until the apples are turning golden. Set aside.

To serve: grill the pizzas on a grill grate over an open fire, or cook them in a large, hot, cast-iron pan for about 3 minutes on each side, until lightly browned. Top with a thin layer of crème pâtissière and the apple mixture, dust with icing sugar and serve hot.

ALMOND CAKE, MEAD ICE CREAM AND CARAMELIZED APPLE

Mead, the alcoholic drink made from fermented honey, was drunk by the Vikings. Today, some microbreweries are producing mead; I think it is a great way of connecting with history.

You will need to make the ice cream at least a day ahead.

Serves 4

Mead ice cream

1 gelatine leaf (2g)
250ml/9fl oz/1 cup whole milk
450ml/16fl oz/2 cups double (heavy) cream
175ml/6fl oz/¾ cup mead
225g/8oz/generous 1 cup caster (superfine) sugar
12 egg yolks
150ml/5fl oz/⅔ cup buttermilk
115g/4oz/½ cup sour cream

Caramelized apple

2–3 Granny Smith apples
450g/1lb/2¼ cups caster (superfine) sugar
90ml/3fl oz/6 tbsp water
85g/3oz/4 tbsp apricot purée
freshly squeezed juice of 1½ lemons

Almond sponge cake

225g/8oz/scant 1 cup egg whites
200g/7oz/1¾ cups icing (confectioners') sugar
85g/3oz/generous ¾ cup almond flour
70g/2½oz/generous ½ cup plain (all-purpose) flour, sifted
150g/5oz/⅔ cup brown butter (see page 58), melted and cooled
½ tsp salt
3 bitter almonds, grated
55g/2oz/4 tbsp butter, melted, for brushing the tins
55g/2oz/scant ½ cup almonds, peeled, to serve

To make the ice cream, soak the gelatine leaf in cold water. Combine the milk, cream, mead, sugar and egg yolks in a saucepan over low heat, constantly stirring with a wooden spoon or rubber spatula, making sure you stir right down to the bottom of the pan. Keep stirring until it thickens slightly, enough to thinly coat the back of the spoon: if you draw a finger across the back of the spoon, it should leave a clear trail. Immediately remove the pan from the heat and place in a chilled bowl. Drain the gelatine from the water, add to the custard and whisk until dissolved. Add the buttermilk and sour cream and leave to cool.

Strain the custard through a fine sieve and leave in the refrigerator for 12 hours. Churn in an ice-cream machine. Store the ice cream in the freezer.

To make the caramelized apple, peel and core the apples and cut each apple in half, if making a large cake, or 16 pieces, if making 4 smaller ones. Put the sugar and water in a saucepan and bring to the boil over medium heat, without stirring. Simmer, without stirring, until the sugar melts and caramelizes. When it is quite dark brown (210°C/410°F on a sugar thermometer), add the apple very carefully to avoid burning your hand. Using a wooden spatula, mix together and simmer for 30 seconds. Add the apricot purée and lemon juice, bring to the boil and mix well. Remove from the heat, cover with a lid and leave for 2 hours without taking the lid off.

Preheat the oven to 180°C/350°F/gas 4. Brush four pie dishes with butter (or use a larger 25cm/10in tin, or cast-iron pan).

To make the almond cake: put the egg whites, icing sugar, almond flour and flour into a bowl and beat until smooth, using an electric whisk. Keep whisking as you add the brown butter a few drops at a time, to emulsify with the batter. Add the salt and grated bitter almonds. Pour the batter into the prepared dishes and bake for about 10 minutes. It is ready when it is slightly risen, but still semi-cooked in the middle.

Top the almond cake with caramelized apple and some of the apple syrup. Grate the almonds on top and serve with mead ice cream.

FIKA

ON FIKA

Do you know what is the bestselling book of all time in Sweden? *The Bible? Fifty Shades of Grey? The Da Vinci Code? Harry Potter?* Nope. In Sweden, the bestseller is called *Seven Kinds of Biscuits* – a recipe book about biscuits. I'm not kidding.

The title derives from the Swedish tradition of serving seven different types of biscuits at the social gathering we call *fika*. *Fika* is one of those concepts that are used to tell the story of Sweden. *Fika* can be simply a cup of coffee and a chat, but in New York you have to fork out eleven dollars for 'the authentic Swedish *fika* experience'. I was at a food festival in England once. A man staggered out of a teepee with the Volvo logo on it and approached me. 'Would you like to experience the Swedish *fika*?' he whispered. It was as if he was some kind of spiritual leader offering to guide me through a seance.

Fika is deeply exoticized but it is also something genuinely Swedish. I take a *fika* break several times a day; I've done it since childhood. I started drinking coffee early. It might not have been one of my parents' best ideas, because I was quite hyper back then as well, but *fika* was a way for me to join in, to sit down with the adults and do what they were doing. In Sweden, *fika* is a way to iron out differences, a way for the employees and the boss to be on the same level. If I were being pretentious, I would call *fika* a symbol of the Swedes' contempt towards hierarchies. I love that trait; we refuse to bow to those in power. As a young chef, when I did work experience at Charlie Trotter's in Chicago and El Bulli in Spain, there was never any *fika*. It was more, *oui chef!* At Ekstedt we start every day with *fika*. One person brews the coffee, another serves rolls or pastries. Then we sit down for *fika*. Many of our best ideas have been born during this kind of undemanding break.

The coffee should be boiled, in my opinion. You add the coffee directly to the water, and you don't use a filter, which gives the coffee a smoother flavour. It's a little bit more of a faff, and you can end up with lumps, but you can't beat the taste. I love coffee and I love chit-chat, therefore I love *fika*.

But it can get a bit over the top, even for me. *Fika* is as close as you can get to an institutionalized mindfulness break in Sweden. You're expected to let everything go and 'just be', which isn't quite my cup

of tea. It's a bit of a joke that I, with my restless temperament, come from Jämtland, the Mecca of *fika*. I can tell you that there, people have *fika* whether it's appropriate or not. If you visit someone in Jämtland, you'll never be able to leave. You can be about to go home, have your car all packed up, engine running, and just as you are saying 'Thanks for everything, see you next time', your host replies, 'Well, I think it's time for us to have *fika*'.

Fika

213

SEVEN BISCUITS

In the early 1900s, seven varieties of biscuits was the ideal when you had guests for afternoon '*fika*' – coffee and cookies. A hostess was thought to be inefficient if she baked fewer than seven varieties and too proud if she baked more. Today we are more relaxed …

SYLTKAKOR
JAM COOKIES

Makes 40–50 cookies

¼ vanilla pod
200g/7oz/generous ¾ cup butter, room temperature
85g/3oz/scant ½ cup caster (superfine) sugar
270g/9½oz/2¼ cups plain (all-purpose) flour
200g/7oz/¾ cup raspberry jam

Preheat the oven to 180°C/350°F/gas 4. Line a baking sheet with baking parchment.

Split the vanilla pod lengthways and scrape out the seeds (save the pod and keep it in a jar with 450g/1lb/2¼ cups sugar to make vanilla sugar, to use in baking).

Put the vanilla seeds, butter, sugar and flour into a food processor and mix briefly to form a dough. Roll the dough into 40–50 balls and place on the baking sheet, leaving 2–3cm/about 1in between each ball. Press your finger onto the dough to create a little hollow and fill it with raspberry jam.

Bake for about 10 minutes until lightly browned. Leave to cool on the baking sheet.

CHOKLADSNITTAR
CHOCOLATE SLICES

Makes 40–50 slices

¼ vanilla pod
200g/7oz/generous ¾ cup butter, room temperature
240g/8½oz/1¼ cups caster (superfine) sugar
300g/10½oz/scant 2½ cups plain (all-purpose) flour
3 tbsp unsweetened cocoa powder
1 tsp baking powder
1 egg, beaten
55g/2oz/5 tbsp nib sugar (pearl sugar)

Preheat the oven to 200°C/400°F/gas 6. Line a baking sheet with baking parchment.

Split the vanilla pod lengthways and scrape out the seeds (save the pod and keep it in a jar with 450g/1lb/2¼ cups sugar to make vanilla sugar, to use in baking).

Beat the butter and sugar together until smooth. Add the flour, cocoa, baking powder and vanilla seeds and work into a dough. Divide into six pieces and shape each piece into a 2cm/¾in diameter roll. Place on the baking sheet, leaving 2cm/¾in between each roll. Flatten the rolls to about 1cm/½in thick. Brush with egg and sprinkle with nib sugar.

Bake for 10–12 minutes. As soon as you remove them from the oven, cut the rolls into 2cm/¾in pieces and leave to cool on the baking sheet.

DRÖMMAR
DREAMS

Makes 40–50 cookies

125g/4½oz/generous ½ cup butter,
    at room temperature
250g/9oz/2 cups plain (all-purpose) flour
1 tsp ammonium carbonate (baker's ammonium)
250g /9oz/1¼ cups caster (superfine) sugar
100ml/3½fl oz/scant ½ cup vegetable oil

Preheat the oven to 150°C/300°F/gas 2. Line a
large baking sheet with baking parchment.

Using an electric mixer, beat the butter until fluffy
and pale, about 5 minutes.

Sift the flour into a bowl, add the ammonium and
sugar and mix together. Add the oil and butter and
mix well until smooth.

Pipe or spoon the batter onto the baking sheet in
4cm/1½ diameter discs, about 1cm/½ in thick:
you will get about 20 cookies on one sheet, so you
will need to cook them in batches.

Bake for 8–10 minutes, until the cookies rise and
dry out – they should remain very pale. Do not
open the door while they are baking, or they will
collapse and create hard cookies.

Leave to cool on the baking sheet.

BRYSSELKEX
RASPBERRY SUGAR
COOKIES

Makes 40–50 cookies

200g/7oz/generous ¾ cup butter,
    at room temperature
100g/3½oz/½ cup caster (superfine) sugar
270g/9½oz/2¼ cups plain (all-purpose) flour
2 tsp freeze-dried raspberries

In a food processor, or by hand, mix the butter,
55g/2oz/¼ cup of the sugar and the flour to
a dough. Wrap in clingfilm and chill in the
refrigerator for 1 hour.

In a food processor, blitz the freeze-dried
raspberries to a powder. Combine with the
remaining sugar.

Divide the dough into four pieces and shape each
piece into a 4cm/1½in diameter log. Roll in the
raspberry sugar and place in the refrigerator for
1 hour.

Preheat the oven to 180°C/350°F/gas 4. Line a
baking sheet with baking parchment.

Cut the dough into 1cm/½in thick slices and place
on the baking sheet, leaving 2–3cm/1in between
each slice.

Bake for 8 minutes until pale golden. Leave to cool
on the baking sheet.

KOLASNITTAR
CARAMEL SLICES

Makes 40–50 slices

¼ vanilla pod
100g/3½oz/scant ½ cup unsalted butter,
   at room temperature
55g/2oz/¼ cup soft brown sugar
6 tsp dark corn syrup [or golden syrup]
150g/5½oz/1¼ cups plain (all-purpose) flour
½ tsp bicarbonate of soda (baking soda)
¼ tsp salt

Preheat the oven to 180°C/350°F/gas 4. Line a baking sheet with baking parchment.

Split the vanilla pod lengthways and scrape out the seeds (save the pod and keep it in a jar with 450g/1lb/2¼ cups sugar to make vanilla sugar, to use in baking).

Beat the butter, sugar, syrup and vanilla seeds together until smooth and airy. Sift together the flour, bicarbonate of soda and salt, and add to the butter mixture, gently working it into a dough. Divide into four pieces and shape each piece into a 2cm/¾in diameter roll. Place on the baking sheet, leaving 2cm/¾in between each roll. Flatten the rolls to about 1cm/½in thick.

Bake for 12–15 minutes. As soon as you remove them from the oven, cut across the rolls into 2cm/¾in pieces and leave to cool on the baking sheet.

FINSKA PINNAR
FINNISH FINGERS

Makes 40–50 fingers

5 bitter almonds
200g/7oz/generous ¾ cup butter,
   at room temperature
30g/1oz/2 tbsp caster (superfine) sugar
270g/9½oz/2¼ cups plain (all-purpose) flour
1 egg, lightly beaten
30g/1oz/2½ tbsp nib sugar (pearl sugar)
30g/1oz/4 tbsp almonds, chopped

Grind the bitter almonds to a powder.

Combine the butter, sugar, flour and ground bitter almonds to a smooth dough. Wrap in clingfilm and chill in the refrigerator for 1 hour.

Preheat the oven to 200°C/400°F/gas 6. Line a baking sheet with baking parchment.

Divide the dough into four pieces and shape each one into a roll about 60cm/2ft long. Place the rolls close to each other on a work surface and brush with the beaten egg, then sprinkle with the nib sugar and chopped almonds. Cut the dough into 4cm/1½in lengths and place on the baking sheet.

Bake for 8–10 minutes until golden brown. Leave to cool on the baking sheet.

KORINTKAKOR CURRANT BISCUITS

Makes 40–50 biscuits

¼ vanilla pod
200g/7oz/generous ¾ cup butter
55g/2oz/¼ cup caster (superfine) sugar
270g/9½oz/generous 2 cups plain (all-purpose) flour
30g/1oz/3 tbsp currants

Split the vanilla pod lengthways and scrape out the seeds (save the pod and keep it in a jar with 450g/1lb/2¼ cups sugar to make vanilla sugar, to use in baking).

Combine the butter, sugar, flour, currants and vanilla seeds to a smooth dough. Wrap in clingfilm and chill in the refrigerator for 1 hour.

Preheat the oven to 180°C/350°F/gas 4. Line a baking sheet with baking parchment.

Roll the dough into 40–50 balls and place on the baking sheet. Using a fork, press the dough lightly to create a ribbed pattern.

Bake for 8–10 minutes until golden brown. Leave to cool on the baking sheet.

HOT CHOCOLATE WITH DRIED ORANGE

A lovely rich and creamy chocolate drink. Ideal for kids, it also works well for adults, topped up with dark rum.

Serves 4

1 litre/1¾ pints/4 cups milk
150g/5oz dark chocolate, chopped
90ml/3fl oz/6 tbsp double (heavy) cream, whipped
1 tsp ground dried orange peel (see page 54)

In a saucepan, heat the milk to the point of boiling, then remove from the heat. Add the chocolate and leave for 1 minute without stirring.

Using a plastic or wooden spoon, stir the milk until the chocolate has dissolved. Serve at once, topped with whipped cream, sprinkled with dried orange peel.

SAFFRON BISCOTTI

One of the typical spices used in Sweden at Christmas is saffron. Using it to flavour these Italian almond cookies makes a delicious combination.

Makes 35 biscuits

pinch of saffron strands
1 tbsp Marsala wine
40g/1½oz/5 tbsp almonds, peeled
115g/4oz/½ cup unsalted butter,
   at room temperature
2 eggs
125g/4½oz/generous 1 cup icing (confectioners')
   sugar
315g/11oz/2½ cups plain (all-purpose) flour, sifted
40g/1½oz baking powder
pinch of salt
vegetable oil for brushing the baking sheet

Soak the saffron in the Marsala.

Preheat the oven to 180°C/350°F/gas 4.

Spread the almonds on a baking sheet and bake for 5 minutes. Remove and leave to cool. Chop roughly.

Using an electric mixer, beat the butter until light and fluffy. With the mixer running, gradually add the eggs, sugar and saffron Marsala and mix thoroughly. Add the flour, baking powder and salt, and combine to form a smooth dough. Finally, stir in the chopped almonds.

Grease a baking sheet with oil.

Divide the dough in half and roll each piece into a log about 2cm/¾in high and 5cm/2in wide. Place on the oiled baking sheet and bake for 30 minutes until golden brown.

Remove from the oven and leave to cool on the baking sheet for 5 minutes. Place on a chopping board and cut diagonally into 2cm/¾in thick slices. Put the slices back on the baking sheet, cut side up. Bake for 5 minutes until golden brown. Turn them over and bake for another 5 minutes. Remove from the oven and leave to cool on the baking sheet.

PEPPARKAKA
GINGER COOKIES WITH BLUE CHEESE

Pepparkaka, in the shape of Christmas trees, hearts or Santa Claus, are traditionally served with *glögg*, or mulled wine (see page 228). I think they are also perfect with blue cheese.

In the late 15th century, King Johan II of Sweden was prescribed ginger cookies by his doctor, to improve his bad temper. Today, the myth endures that children will be nicer and behave better if they eat *pepparkaka*. And nice children might get more Christmas presents…

The dough needs to rest for 24 hours before you roll and shape it.

Makes approx. 150 cookies

200g/7oz/generous ¾ cup unsalted butter
150g/5oz/scant ½ cup dark corn syrup,
    or golden syrup
175g/6oz/generous ¾ cup soft brown sugar,
    or muscovado sugar
150ml/5fl oz/⅔ cup double (heavy) cream
600g/1lb 5oz/5 cups plain (all-purpose) flour,
    plus extra for dusting
3 tsp bicarbonate of soda (baking soda)
3 tsp ground ginger
3 tsp ground cinnamon
1½ tsp ground cloves
1½ tsp ground cardamom
280g/10oz blue cheese, to serve

Put the butter, syrup and sugar in a saucepan over medium heat until the sugar has dissolved. Place in a food processor, add the cream and mix until smooth.

Sift the flour together with the bicarbonate of soda and spices. Add the flour to the butter mixture and mix in a food processor to make a smooth dough. Wrap the dough in clingfilm and leave in the refrigerator for 24 hours.

Preheat the oven to 200°C/400°F/gas 6. Line a baking sheet with baking parchment.

On a floured work surface, roll out the dough to about 4mm/just under ¼in thick. Using a shaped cutter, a mould or a knife, cut out the cookies and place on the baking sheet.

Bake for about 5 minutes. Leave to cool on the baking sheet. Serve with your favourite blue cheese.

GLÖGG
MULLED WINE

Glögg is a sweet Swedish version of mulled wine, served at Christmas with almonds and raisins.

Makes 1.4 litres / 2½ pints / 6 cups

120g/4oz/⅔ cup caster (superfine) sugar
900ml/1¼ bottles/3¾ cups red wine
2 cinnamon sticks
8 cloves
2 cardamom pods
4 pieces of orange peel, about 5cm/2in each
150ml/5fl oz/⅔ cup vodka
150ml/5fl oz/⅔ cup cognac

Put the sugar in a cast-iron or heavy-based saucepan over a medium–high heat until the sugar dissolves and caramelizes to a light brown colour.

Add all the remaining ingredients and heat to 60–70°C/140–160°F. Keep at this temperature for 30 minutes.

Serve warm, or leave to cool and store in a sealed bottle.

CAMOMILE TEA

Dried camomile flowers make a fresh-tasting tea; serve with honey and freshly squeezed lemon juice to taste.

Makes 1.4 litres / 2½ pints / 6 cups

1.4 litres/2½ pints/6 cups water
6 tsp dried camomile flowers

Heat the water to 80°C/175°F. Put the camomile flowers in a large jug or bowl and add 900ml/ 32fl oz/3¾ cups of the water. Leave to infuse for 5 minutes.

Add the remaining water and strain into jug before serving.

INDEX

ACKNOWLEDGEMENTS

Thanks to Thomas Eidefors, Rod Pérez, Emily, Laura, Liz and Max, and the rest of the team at Pavilion. This book was one of the most fun projects I've done, thanks to you!

SUPPLIERS

Commercial fire pits:
www.weberbbq.co.uk

Flambadou (flamboir à lard):
www.uniqus.se (Sweden)
www.tompess.com (France)
www.blenheimforge.co.uk (UK; will make to order)

EKSTEDT